TRAMP TO QUEEN

CAPTAIN
JOHN TREASURE JONES

Edited by Richard J. Tennant

TEMPUS

First published 2008

Tempus Publishing
Cirencester Road, Chalford,
Stroud, Gloucestershire, GL6 8PE
www.thehistorypress.co.uk

Tempus Publishing is an imprint of The History Press

British Library Cataloguing in Publication Data.
A catalogue record for this book is available from the British Library.

ISBN 978 0 7524 4625 7

Typesetting and origination by The History Press
Printed in Great Britain by Ashford Colour Press Ltd., Gosport, Hants.

CONTENTS

FOREWORD

Over eighty-five years have passed since Captain John Treasure Jones set foot on his first ship. In 1921, he joined the 4,785-ton tramp steamer *Grelgrant* moored in Cardiff Docks and within a few hours was covered in coal dust. He found himself in conditions a far cry from those at home so he could have been forgiven for thoughts of turning his back on any ideas of going to sea and returning home to the family farm. However, his family nautical ties and ambition held fast and he set forth on a career that would lead him to the command of one of the greatest and favourite liners – the *Queen Mary*.

This book will take the reader through a voyage of time from the captain's days as an apprentice through his service in the Royal Naval Reserve during times of conflict, serving in a variety of ships and the long haul up the promotion ladder to command. It is the story of a distinguished captain who not only had to be an expert seaman but one who had to care for thousands of passengers and at the same time encourage his officers and crew to live up to the glowing reputation of ships of the Cunard Line.

An important chapter in this book for marine historians and passenger ship aficionados is the story of the *Queen Mary*'s final voyage to California. While the captain was sad that his ship was being sold, he was very proud to be in command for the final trip. I am sure if he were alive today, he would be equally proud of the affection still extended to the ship and the determination of her owners and supporters to preserve her for future generations.

Most of the words in this book are the personal recollections of Captain Treasure Jones and would probably have remained unpublished if his son-in-law had not taken it upon himself to collate the notes and research other aspects of his life to complete the story. *Tramp to Queen* records a rich tapestry of life at sea on the great ocean liners and I congratulate Richard Tennant for his important contribution to maritime and Cunard Line history.

Commodore R. W. Warwick
Somerset, September 2007

NOTE ON THE TEXT

The material in this book has been collected from the personal papers of Captain John Treasure Jones and edited together by Richard J. Tennant, his son-in-law. Tennant's editorial notes are interspersed throughout the book and are presented in *italics*.

ACKNOWLEDGEMENTS

I would like to extend my thanks to Mr S.J. Spear, Naval Secretary (Honours and Awards), in the Office of the Naval Secretary, Portsmouth, for his assistance in tracing and explaining the details of John's decorations and medals. The Directorate of Personnel Support (Navy) was also most forthcoming with details of his service records.

I am also indebted to Dr David Jenkins, Senior Curator at the National Waterfront Museum, Swansea, for his encouragement, support, and additional background information.

I need to thank Mr David F. Hutchings. He had met John on several occasions during his retirement and interviewed him for background information to include in his book *RMS Queen Mary, Fifty Years of Splendour*, as well as several others about the various Cunard Liners. Having been through the publication process himself, David was willing and able to share invaluable advice and information in this respect. His network of contacts also managed to find some of the more elusive photographs.

Kenneth Vard produced a rather special book entitled *Liners in Art*, full of wonderful paintings of the memorable great liners. Ken and the captain spent many happy hours together over the years, both before and after John's retirement, and he has been most kind in allowing me to reproduce many of the paintings in his book.

I am also extremely grateful to Stephen Card who has kindly allowed me to reproduce his paintings from *Liners in Art*, as well as from his splendid and highly recommended book *Cunarders*.

My wife and I have been friends with Jan Chris and Tineke Cleyndert for quite some time, as a result of having lived in the Netherlands for a number of years. It was something of a surprise, therefore, to only recently find out that he not only knew the places and even some of the people mentioned in the text about Indonesia, but that his family had lived on the same street. He was most helpful in correcting the Dutch spellings and terminology.

Commodore Ron Warwick, himself the author of a couple of books, has been most helpful with advice and support, besides providing some valuable background information. I would also like to particularly thank him for writing the foreword for the book. He represents the last link in the chain of history – his father, Bill Warwick took the first command of *QE2* at the time that John's career and that of the *Queen Mary* were coming to a close, and Ron recently completed his career as the first master of *QM2*.

I count myself very fortunate that it was Campbell McCutcheon who reacted so promptly to the synopsis I circulated around the publishers. Essentially he is a very keen and knowledgeable liner historian. What has also proved to be a substantial additional bonus is that his wife, Janette, is equally enthusiastic and has at least five books on the great Cunard liners to her credit. They have been most generous in making available from their private collection many additional illustrations so as to enable us to bring the colour section up to an unprecedented full thirty-two pages.

Lately I have been very fortunate in being so well supported by Jenny Lawson, who has worked tirelessly through the nitty-gritty of the editorial process to bring the book to its final stages.

The captain's sons, Michael, David and Robert, and his daughter, my wonderful wife Susan, have all been very patient and long-suffering in trawling through cases, boxes and files in order to satisfy my requests for more family information, pictures and documents.

৯ ৯ ৯

ILLUSTRATION ACKNOWLEDGEMENTS

Haverfordwest Town Museum (HTM), Mr Simon Hancock

Pembrokeshire County Library (PCL), Local Studies Collection, Ms Sue Armour

Mrs Margaret Davies, Cuckoo Mill Farm, Pelcomb Bridge, Haverfordwest

Brian S. John (BSJ), for photos from *Old Pembrokeshire Photographs 1873-1934*

Paul Munt, Haverfordwest

David F. Hutchings (DFH)

Central Library Cardiff (CLC), Ms Katrina Coopey

Imperial War Museum (IWM) London, Mr Alan Wakefield

National Maritime Museum (NMM) Woolwich, Mr Jeremy Michell

National Waterfront Museum (NWM) Swansea, Dr David Jenkins

National Museums Liverpool (NML) Maritime Archives, Ms Anne Gleave

Tyne and Wear Archive Service (TWAS)

Mission to Seafarers (MTS) London, Ms Ann Haines

Luis Photos, Gibraltar (LP), Mrs M.A. Mascarenhas

Janette & Campbell McCutcheon (JCM)

Lymington Library, Ms Kathryn Thomas

Kenneth Vard (KV)

Stephen J. Card (SJC)

CHAPTER 1

THE GROWING YEARS

It was 6 a.m. on 18 August 1905, the sun had just risen over the distant trees in blaze of glory and there were the makings of a beautiful summer's day. The birds were singing and the cocks crowing to welcome another day.

Though it was early in the day there was already considerable hustle and bustle and comings and goings in the home of Shrewsbury and Margaret Treasure Jones; a three-bedroomed house, named Cuckoo Mill, about two miles from the small, but important, town of Haverfordwest in Pembrokeshire, Wales.

New life was stirring on the forty-five acre small farm which Shrewsbury ran as a side line to his hay and corn business. The new life was not in the sheds amongst the animals; rather it was in the house, up in the bedroom. Margaret, his wife, was expecting her second child and labour pains were starting. Shrewsbury (known as 'Shewy' to all his friends) was sent post-haste across the stream and meadow to the local inn, where Martha the midwife lived, a matter of only a quarter of a mile. Whilst he was on his errand, the maid was stoking the fire and boiling the water ready for the forthcoming event. The two children, Hugh, by his late wife, and Irene, seventeen months old, were still asleep upstairs. It was not long before Martha arrived and took charge. The roosters had not long finished their morning chorus when a new sound, though as old as Adam, was heard; the cries of a new-born babe. Thus arrived into this exciting world a male child who was later christened John Treasure Jones and sixty years later was to receive a certain degree of publicity as the last captain of the finest passenger liner ever to sail the oceans, *Queen Mary*.

This part of the country was known as 'Little England beyond Wales' due to the fact that scarcely anyone in the southern part of Pembrokeshire spoke or understood any of the Welsh language; yet in the northern part of the county, Welsh was the everyday language. The only time one would hear Welsh spoken in Haverfordwest was on the weekly market and monthly fair days when farmers from all over the county brought their produce and livestock to town to sell, and to make their weekly purchases in the shops.

There were no motor cars in those days; live horse power was the means of transport and power in other ways. Here one could see some of the finest horses, hunters and ponies in the country. People used to vie with each other to see who had the smartest, fastest pony, or cob and trap, or governors' car. It was a treat for the eyes to watch them come into town on Market Days, and driving to church or chapel on Sundays.

My earliest recollections are of being taken to the local country school about one and a half miles away, at the age of three and a half years. I was carried a good part of the way by my step-brother Hugh who was eight years older than me; sometimes we were driven in the pony and trap. I therefore seemed to have started school at a very young age. There were no school buses or taxis or cars to take us to school, so it was either walk or go by horse. There was little danger on the roads in those days; the only traffic we met was the odd horse and trap or farm cart, the very occasional pedal cycle and other pedestrians.

What fun we had on the farm at that early age, especially in the summer and at haymaking time. In those days every farmer brewed his own beer, so that there was always plenty of it in

Fair at St Clears, *c.*1900. (BSJ)

Haverfordwest, Scotchwell, no date. (PCL)

Opposite above: Cuckoo Mill Farmhouse.

Opposite below: Haverfordwest, Cattle Fair on St Thomas Green, *c.*1905. (HTM)

Haverfordwest, Tabernacle Choir outing to Dale 1912. (PCL)

Haverfordwest, Bridgend Square, no date. (PCL)

Haverfordwest, Prendergast, pre-1921. (PCL)

the cellars. We children were allowed to have a little of this from quite an early age. During the haymaking the men were given all the beer they wanted to drink as it was hot, dusty, thirsty work. This proved to be my downfall one day. I had wandered up the field close to the house from where they were leading in the hay and the men gave me quite a lot of this beer to drink. I was about four years old at the time and I can remember what I drank it out of, and where in the field, as if it was only yesterday. The beer used to be carried up to the fields on one or two gallon galvanised cans with lids on them, and the lid used to be used as the utensil to drink out of. I can well remember drinking out of this by a gateway in the hedge. I staggered home down the field and ended up by falling into the tub of pig-swill, kitchen waste liquid, kept outside the back-kitchen door. My cries brought the maid who duly rescued me and took me to my alarmed mother, who washed me down and put me to bed. I cannot recollect whether she realised that her four–year–old son was well and truly pickled. I often wonder how anyone can recollect being drunk at such an early age. I did not rush to sign the pledge the next day, but I think my ration of beer was cut down!

A year or two later we moved to a much larger house on the outskirts of a little country village named Portfield Gate; this village boasted two inns, called The Penry Arms and The New Inn, and also a small shop and post office combined. The family in the post office had been there for a few generations and, as far as I am aware, it is still being run by the same family.

There was a carpenter's shop and the blacksmith's shop. Both of these used to fascinate us children and used to draw us there like a magnet would iron filings. We spent a great deal of time in and around these shops, watching the carpenter, David Absalom, and the blacksmith, Ben James. Though we must have been a nuisance to them both many times, I do not recall them ever being unkind or nasty to us, though at times we used to tease Ben and sometimes had to make a quick getaway to escape his wrath or feigned wrath. I used to love blowing the bellows for him and watch him heat and hammer the hot metal into the required shape either for horseshoes or steel wheel-bands and various other things. Farmers used to come from far

Working on the fields, 1884. (HTM)

Working on the fields. 1898. (BSJ)

Opposite: Working on the fields cutting hay, near Boncath, no date. (PCL)

and wide to have their horse shod with Ben. When I grew a little older, I used to take Dad's horses to him and watch him shoe them; light shoes for the race horses and heavier ones for the working horses. I loved the smell of the burning hooves as he fitted them. Having hammered them into the required shape, he would then quickly cool them in water and nail them on with great expertise. For David Absalom I liked turning the wet-stone when he sharpened his tools and, when permitted, used to watch him plane and chisel the wood for the various things he made. Cartwheels were one of the things he spent a lot of time making and repairing, also farm gates. The smell of the shaven wood was perfume to my nostrils. Ben and David were two entirely different characters; they were both great old characters in their different ways.

Ben was a tall, heavily bearded man who looked as if he seldom ever washed and was seldom out of his smithy clothes and leather apron. The few times I can recollect seeing him dressed in his Sunday best he always looked awkward and uncomfortable and still had that 'sooty smithy' look about him. He loved his pint of beer and lived alone; I think he must have been a bachelor.

David Absalom always looked clean, drank very little, if at all and was a regular at the local Wesleyan chapel, where the lady schoolteacher, Miss Pewsey, played the organ and took Sunday school and various lay-preachers used to come and preach on Sunday evenings.

There was 'Jones the Postmaster', a white bearded small man who had been postmaster there for along time and was a respected old boy, liked by most of the villagers. Then there was the Thomas family who lived in the big house in the village, while on the other side of the village was the Scurlock family, second cousins of ours, who worked a small farm alongside the chapel and had a milk round in Haverfordwest.

All we children from the village went to Sutton School which was situated not in the village but about one and a half miles away, near a couple of farms and cottages, not large enough to be called a village. The children from the farms all around for miles attended this school and most of them had to walk all the way.

The school was run by two lady teachers, Miss Ellen Owen, who came from Nolton, where her people ran a sizable farm, the other was Miss Pewsey, who lived in the Schoolhouse. She was a tall, imposing-looking woman, but there was no doubt who was the headmistress – that was Miss Owen. I spent some happy years there up to the age of nine, when my mother bought me a bicycle and I went to school in Haverfordwest. This was a much bigger school with far more pupils who mostly came from the town. This was very different from the country school. This also was a distance of about one-and a half miles

The previous winter I was grievously ill with pneumonia. In those days more people died from it than recovered, and I was almost one of those who died. My aunt Mary came from Pembroke Dock to nurse me and used to sleep in the same room as me. She was a marvellous lady for whom I had great affection; she died in her nineties and up to the last insisted on living alone. Our family doctor, Dr Williams, was a kindly man and had done all he could for me. I well remember the hot linseed poultices they used to wrap around my chest and lungs, the black ointment they rubbed on my chest, the horrible iron and quinine medicine I had to take regularly and the masses of oranges I sucked. On one visit he told my mother that he did not think I would get better, that the crisis would come at any moment and that she could let me have whatever I liked for supper. Believe it or not, though I was supposed to be dying, I wanted home-brewed beer and pickled onions for my supper that night. With much trepidation from my mother, I was allowed to have them and I ate and must have enjoyed them. During the night I became violently sick and started to vomit up the fluid and phlegm from my chest and lungs. This was the crisis and the turning point, and from then on I started to recover and was nursed back to health. Doctor Williams used to swear that home-brewed beer and pickled onions saved my life; mind, he had a twinkle in his eye and a big grin on his face when he said this. Perhaps it did. But these days there are quicker and surer methods to cure pneumonia.

Our family had increased fairly regularly and I now had three sisters and two brothers, in addition to my step-brother Hugh. After me came Robert, eighteen months later. He was a thrifty type and saved his pennies; I used to spend mine in the village shop. I well recall an escapade which got me into trouble.

The Fair had come to Haverfordwest and among the amusements was a movie picture tent. Sidney Thomas, from the village, who was the same age as me, persuaded me to convince my brother Robert to bring his money box out; we then persuaded him to let us open it and we would all three go into town and see the moving pictures. This happened at the quarry behind the blacksmith's shop. Having done this, we three set off for town, duly arrived at the Fair and stood outside the tent waiting for it to open. We had been waiting there for quite a long time when, who should show up on the back of the pony 'Munt' (named after the jeweller from whom Dad had bought her), than Jack Harris, one of Dad's men who lived in. Somehow or other my mother had found out where we had headed for and sent him to find us. Robert and I were bundled on to the back of the pony with Jack holding tightly on to him.

Sidney was left to find his own way home, and at home we were taken for the reckoning, and we had not even seen our movie! On arrival home I had to face the music which resulted in me having a slipper on my rear. I always started to yell before I felt the first; this way I figured that I would not have so many. Except for a few pennies with which we had bought some sweets, Robert had his money back.

In those days our efforts to get to see the movies did not meet with much success. A friend of my mother's, a Miss Jenkins, had spent a day or two with us and was to be driven back in the governors' car Saturday evening. There was a movie showing in town that evening and as a treat, my mother was allowing Rene, Robert and I to go and see it with our elder brother, Hugh, who was to drive the governors' car. Our pony, 'Munt', was a bit wild and had a habit, as soon as she was out of the drive and onto the road, of tearing off at a very fast trot and, if you did not restrain her, she would be off at a gallop. Now Saturday was the day most farmers went into town and had a day out, many imbibing perhaps a little too freely, but their horses

Haverfordwest, Bostock's Fair, *c.*1900. (HTM)

always knew the way home once they were headed in the right direction. It was a very dark night when we left home, so it must have been in the winter time, and as soon as the pony was turned for town she was off at top speed. We had not gone further then the blacksmith's shop which was about fifty yards down the road, when there was an almighty crash and over we went. I found myself pinned down by the wing of the governors' car, but as it was fairly light I was able to wriggle out from under it. Fortunately no one received any injuries other than a scratch and bruise, but Miss Jenkins, who must have been around sixty, was quite shocked and upset. We all returned to the house and licked our wounds, and that was the end of our trip to town to see the movies.

Apparently we had collided with one of the farmers who had had too good a day in town and was asleep in his trap with no lights on, with the pony taking him home. He and his trap, which was of a much heavier type than our light governors' car, came to no harm and proceeded on his way without knowing quite what had occurred. He happened to be a distant relation of ours. Our pony had disappeared, the shafts had broken off when we overturned and the pony continued into town with the shafts still attached until he came to the King's Arms where we normally stabled her whenever we went into town. They, naturally, were somewhat worried. The ostler brought the pony home and found out what had happened.

My father was a great sportsman; he loved his hunting, shooting and cricket, besides his club life; I gather that he was also was no mean billiard player. He appeared to be very popular and I suppose, by the standards of those days, reasonably well-off. We lived in what could be called a gentleman's country house of modest size with three big bedrooms and a maid's room, plus a water closet upstairs. This was real luxury in those days, but there was no bathroom, nor any hot or cold running water in the house other than a tap in the back kitchen which drew water from a large galvanised tank which collected rainwater from the roof. There was, of course, no electric lighting and the house was lit by oil lamps and candles. This was usual in those days, at least in the country, and we thought nothing of it. We fetched our drinking water from a communal village well about a quarter of a mile away on the other side of the village. It was beautiful drinking water and we often used to drink from the well on our way to and from

Haverfordwest High Street, *c.*1895. Note the governors' car, the cobbled street surface and the gas lamp-post. In the left foreground is Bisley Munts's shop, which is still the family business to this day. (Munt)

school at Sutton. As we grew older it was our job to go and draw the drinking water for the house in galvanised two-gallon cans. There was a water pump in the back yard, the water from which we used for washing and for the animals, but as it was a farmyard, we did not consider it really fit for humans to drink, though we used to sometimes.

We kept one maid, who lived in and helped in the house and with the milking. I believe she was paid about thirty pounds a year and she lived with the family but ate in the kitchen, where we mostly ate except when we had visitors. It was usual for these maids to have only one night a week off at this time. Our maid stayed with us for many years.

The farm-help was engaged by the year at Michaelmas time *(29 September)*, when the Fair that month was known as Portfield Fair and was the hiring fair. All the farmers and help came to town that day and there farmers took on their help for the following year. There was an amusement fair at the same time and it was THE event of the year for the country folk. Many a country wench 'got into trouble' that night on the way home!

Bathing was a Saturday night ritual in those days for us youngsters. The big boiler in the back kitchen used to be filled up with water from the pump and the fire lit under it. It was my job mostly to stoke it up. We bathed in a portable galvanised bath which used to be placed in front of the kitchen fire for warmth, and we had our Saturday night treat there. In spite of having plenty of cats around there were always lots of mice around the kitchens and pantries; they especially liked the warmth around the kitchen fire. One Saturday night when I was having my bath, I spotted a mouse tail sticking out of one of the holes. I could reach it from my bath. I managed to catch it by its tail and, little murderer that I was, drowned it in the bath. The thought of doing such a thing now would be repulsive to me.

My father kept quite a lot of horses. As well as the work horses for the wagons to transport the hay and corn, he kept four or five hunters, hurdlers and steeplechasers. He employed a local man to look after and exercise them, and trained them himself. He used to send them as far afield as Worcester to race. I loved these horses and used to help the groom with them

Haverfordwest, Cattle Fair, no date. (PCL)

Haverfordwest, Scotchwell, *c.*1908. (PCL)

Haverfordwest, Milford Road – Coronation celebrations, 1910. (PCL)

Haverfordwest Carnival, in Victoria Place and High Street, *c.*1905. (HTM)

from an early age. I often used to ride the pony bareback but never ventured on the hunters and blood horses.

This was great hunting country; Pembrokeshire boasted two Fox Hunts with another close by in Carmarthen. Twice a week during the season one could hear the calls of 'tallyho' and the cry of the hounds on the scent, when the country Squires and many more prosperous farmers, and even some of the town businessmen, mounted their hunters and thrilled to the chase over the big Pembrokeshire banks and across the fields, while everyone in the vicinity stopped work to watch them go by. Here were some of the finest weight carrying hunters in Britain and some of the finest horsemen. Amongst the latter was Shewy Jones; he was well known and liked for his daring riding over this difficult country. There was not much he did not know about horses and he liked nothing better than to be in the saddle on a beautiful seventeen-hand hunter.

In the family collection is a fine solid silver punch bowl. The wooden display base is inscribed:

> *P. H.C. Point to Point 7th April 1910*
> *Presented by Lord Kensington*
> *Farmers Race*
> *Won by*
> *Mr S. T. Jones' Slippery*
> *Owner up*

I well remember the first time I left home for a holiday. I had never been away from my mother overnight before. It was the summer after I had been very ill and nearly died. It was 1914 and I was not quite nine years old. My sister Irene and I were going to Barry by train to spend a few weeks' holiday with our grandparents and aunts at thirty-two The Parade, Barry. We had never been in a train before, so it was terribly exciting.

Haverfordwest, Scotchwell, Hunt, 1923. (PCL)

We were driven in to the station by our mother and we could hardly wait for the train to pull into the station, but once the train had pulled out and mother had disappeared from view, I started to feel very lonely. But there were so many exciting new things to see that I forgot about mother for a while. Rene and I hardly sat down at all. We spent most of the time looking out of the windows and for the first few times were quite scared when trains rushed past us in the opposite direction. We were met at Cardiff by our aunts Beaty and Lil, who took us into another train for Barry. As we passed from Barry Dock to Barry we saw for the first time the big ships in the docks; there seemed to be hundreds of them and this was a treat for us. Not long later we arrived at Barry and walked from the station to my grandparents' house which was about half a mile away. The Parade looked out over the bay to the Bristol Channel; it was a fine view from there as we walked up the road. I was somewhat overcome when I met my grandparents as at first they looked awe inspiring to me. Grandpa Williams with a big bushy white beard and balding head, but he had a nice twinkle in his eye and a soft pleasant voice. Grandma was a broadish, rather stern-looking woman in a black voluminous dress, who welcomed me with a hug and a smile. My two aunts, I thought, looked beautiful. I suppose they must have been about thirty at that time. They had a lovely home with all sorts of beautiful things from abroad.

This was a most exciting and eventful day, not only for me, but for the country, and possibly the world; it was 14 August and war was declared against Germany in response to their sending their army into Belgium. I am sure that if war had been declared a day earlier, I should never have been allowed to leave home for Barry.

By the evening I was feeling homesick and was soon in tears. When I was tucked up in a nice clean bed that evening I went to sleep wishing I was back home with mum and the other children. But a good night's sleep and the sun shining the next morning, with the prospect of all sorts of new things to see soon got rid of my homesickness. There were so many things to do and see. Most exciting of all was watching the ships going up and down the channel

Haverfordwest, Queens Hotel & Railway Station, *c.*1900. (PCL)

through grandpa's very large telescope which he had mounted on the balcony on the first floor. I spent hours doing this and grandpa telling me all about them and relating some stories of his life at sea to me. This, I have no doubt, sowed the seeds which later made me determined to go to sea and become a captain myself. He, grandpa, was a retired sailing ship captain. He used to keep me spellbound with these stories about the sea and foreign lands. Then there were all the amusements at Barry Island and the bathing and rambling at Cold Knap and Pebbly Beach, also the boat racing at the rowing club. My aunt Lil used to do a lot of that.

All too soon the holiday was over and we were put in the train for home, and it was back to school; but Barry and the ships were treasured memories. I had met a nice young girl named Nora Wilkins who lived in the Parade. She, her brother and Rene and I used to spend quite a lot of time together on the beaches. I was to go back to Barry for summer holidays frequently after this. My aunt Lil still lives there and I frequently visit her and often meet Nora who visits there once a week.

The war was gaining momentum; the Battle of Mons was over and the papers full of 'The Angels of Mons' and how they had seemingly stopped the German Uhlans from completely massacring our troops that day. I was at a very impressionable age and in my mind I can still see the pictures and stories that were printed in the press and magazines after it.

The war affected us all in some way, some more than others. My step-brother Hugh, who was in the Territorials, was soon called up. As he knew a great deal about horses, he was placed in the transport division of the Welsh Regiment. This entailed handling mules. He had no previous experience of these animals and found them very different to the horses. It was not long before he learnt what the expression 'as stubborn as a mule' meant and, as he was often on the receiving end of their hoofs, he learnt to respect them.

My dad was forty when the war started and, although he was a member of the Pembrokeshire Yeomanry, because of his business he was employed as a government-agent purchasing hay and corn and horses from the farmers in Pembrokeshire for the army. Much of this was compulsory sales, after allowing the farmer to keep enough for his needs on the farm for his own consumption. For this purpose he hired from my uncle, Percy Wilkins, a chauffeur driven Model T Ford twice a week. During my holidays I used to go with him round the farms. This was my first experience of riding in a car and I enjoyed every minute of it.

At the age of twelve I gained a scholarship to Haverfordwest Grammar School; this was considered one of the best schools in west Wales at the time. There were boarders from as far afield as Cardiff. My father had been a pupil in this school and, as it happened, my three sons were also pupils there.

I am afraid I was not very academic in those days, but loved my football and cricket; the school did not play rugby football in those days. I used to spend an hour most evenings after school practising on the playing fields with the boarders and some of the town boys, as the playing field was on my route home. I used a bicycle as transport and this reminds me of my early days with my bike. I remember the day mother purchased it at my uncle's in Dew Street, just below where we stabled the horse. It was a Saturday and the town was full of farmers with their horses and traps. Although I could ride a bike, I had to climb on alongside a wall or something, or be put on, and when stopping, I had to get off the same way. I was put on the bike outside the shop and started off up the street, but when I came level with the pub where the horses were stabled there was no room for me to pass through and I well remember running into a portly farmer who, in no uncertain terms, told me what he thought of me. Someone put me back on my mount and I reached home without any further incident.

I never recall my parents chastising me for being late coming home from school, though I am sure my homework suffered for it; I always did my written work, but I am afraid my reading work was somewhat neglected.

When I started in the Grammar School, the six of us who topped the list in the county entrance examination were place in the third form, whilst the others were in the second. We in the third were flung straight into many new subjects – Latin, French, Chemistry, Geometry,

Haverfordwest, Prendergast School, *c.*1914. (PCL)

Haverfordwest Grammar School and Fish Market, Dew Street, *c.*1910. (HTM)

Algebra, etc. I found difficulty in absorbing so many new subjects, though I quite liked French, Latin and Maths.

The Headmaster, Mr Hooper, used to take us for Latin that first year. He was a tall, smart, good-looking and imposing man, with a sarcastic turn of wit. We were all somewhat scared of him and he liked cracking jokes at our expense. Seated next to me was Price Jones and, with my name Treasure, we were often a target for his jokes with such expressions as 'Never a Treasure without a Price', or, if Price was missing, 'You are a Priceless Treasure today'. These used to cause titters around the form.

I was always struggling, but was somewhere around the middle of the form for position. After a year I was upgraded with most of the others to the fourth form, but I am sure it would have been better for me to have done two years in the third form and achieved a better grounding in the new subjects before going on into the fourth. The result was that I failed to pass the Junior Central Welsh Board Examination at the end of my first year in the fourth, thus having to remain in the fourth for another year. This rather shattered my ego, but looking back it was the best thing that could have happened to me at the time, though I did not think so then. From then on I never failed an examination. From struggling to try and get into the top half of the form I found I had a much better grasp of the subjects and became top of the form, winning the form prize at the end of the second year. The prize was a bound volume of Shakespeare's Plays which I am proud of. I now had much more confidence in myself and never looked back. By the time I left school I was around the top of the fifth form.

The war increased my desire to make the Sea my career. Two uncles, Jack and Harry, were master mariners and officers in the Royal Naval Reserve, and thus were in the Royal Navy during the war years. Uncle Jack had command of 'Q' boats, which were decoys for the U Boats. He was awarded the Distinguished Service Order for his exploits. These two uncles often used to visit us when their ships put into Milford Haven, and go shooting with my father and his friends. They were my heroes. They always looked so smart and handsome in their uniforms, with their gold braid and the ladies clamouring after them. On top of that, they always seemed to have plenty of money, giving me half crowns *(12.5p in decimal currency)* when they left. This was quite a lot of money to me then. This, I thought, is the life for me! I was thirteen years old when the war ended, but by then I was determined to make the sea my life. The one thing that has firmly remained in my mind about the end of the war was meeting my brother, Hugh, returning from the war when I was on my way to school. The last we had heard from him was that he was in Mesopotamia. I could hardly believe my eyes and cried for joy. I was late getting to school that morning, but when I explained why to my Headmaster all was forgiven and he told me I could have the day off. We were one of the luckier families; we did not suffer any war casualties.

Life at the farm as a youngster was interesting, but not easy. It is funny, but while youngsters usually want to ape their elders, at least when they are very young; they usually go in the opposite way once they are in their later teens. So, when I saw the men and women milking the cows, driving, grooming and bedding down the horses and feeding them, I was keen to emulate them and do it myself. Then came the day when I was able to do these things fairly well, and then came the snag. The interest in doing it faded, but now that I could do these things I found I had to continue to do so. It was not long before I was milking five cows before going to school in the morning, giving the horses their final feed and bedding them down in the evenings, and in the summer holidays out in the fields helping with the haymaking and harvesting, and also helping to till the ground. All this was not too bad in the summer, but on the cold winter mornings it was a real chore which I did not enjoy, but could not get out of. We milked in the open and used to literally freeze with the cold at times. On top of that, sometimes the darn cow would let out a kick and knock me off my stool and upset the pail of milk. My favourite job was driving the horse-rake during the haymaking. I often used to do this for some of our neighbouring farmers and earn half a crown and sometimes five shillings *(25p in decimal)* a day for it.

I cannot recollect at what precise age I was allowed to use Dad's shotgun to go shooting rabbits, but it must have been about the age of thirteen or even younger as I was doing it for some years before I went to sea. Catching rabbits became the main source of my pocket money. I bought my own cartridges but sometimes used Dad's without replacing them. I also bought a ferret and nets and my younger brother Robert and I used to go rabbiting with these. I have known us catch as many as twenty-four rabbits in an afternoon. At half a crown a time we did well for pocket money. Sometimes, though, the old ferret would catch and kill the rabbit in the burrow and stay there. We then had a boring profitless afternoon waiting for the ferret to finish his sleep and come out.

Above: Haverfordwest High Street – now with a garage. (PCL)

Opposite: Haverfordwest, river from Parade, *c.*1900. (PCL)

This was not the only source of pocket money. We were in the moleskin business; moleskins were very popular for coats in those days. We bought a few dozen mole traps and caught moles on our and our neighbour's farms for nothing. We skinned them, stretched them on boards to dry and cure, and then sent the pelts away to a firm in Oldham, who would give us up to three shillings for a good pelt.

In the summer, on Friday evenings, I would take the gun and plenty ammunition over to a neighbouring farm where my cousin Tom was learning farming and there were plenty of rabbits; we would go shooting and had some good hauls. Tom and I used to go to town on Saturday evenings, where his mother lived and ran the ironmongers business in the main street. We usually met up with some farmers' daughters and would take them to the cinema, often buying them a box of chocolates and then walking them miles home after. It usually meant another long walk back home, but we thought nothing of this in those days. We never had the courage to kiss them 'good night' either; if we had tried we should probably had our faces slapped.

I well remember the first time I ever kissed a girl. I think I must have been fifteen at the time, as it was not long before I went to sea. I then had a terrific crush on a second cousin of mine, named Daisy John. Her people farmed a large farm called Lambston Hall, about three miles from where we lived. She was the babe of quite a large family of three boys and five girls. About the only times we met were the rare occasions when I went to their Baptist church (which was not often as I was brought up chiefly in the Church of England) or when we met rehearsing for our country concerts in the Sutton schoolroom since we both took part in these concerts.

I used to blacken my face and try to sing funny songs and Daisy usually took part in a sketch. The rehearsals were great fun and that is when I saw the most of my heart-throb. I often used to bring along a box of chocolates for her, thanks to the rabbits and moles, and then ask to walk her home afterwards. This went on for a year or two before I went to sea and I think it was the last time I walked her home that I plucked up the courage to kiss her. It was not a kiss of passion but I shall never forget it; it was a kiss of tenderness, but what an electrifying effect it had on me. I tingled from the top of my head to the end of my toes. It was as if I had been suddenly wafted into heaven. I only had that one light kiss, but I walked home on air and it took me some time before I had my feet on the ground again. I never again recollect a kiss having such an effect on me. We must have been both on the right wavelength at the time.

Though we wrote occasionally after I went to sea and although we did meet once or twice again, we slowly drifted apart. Daisy was a few years older than me and it was not many years later that she married a charming Pembrokeshire man with a wonderful singing voice and raised a family. But I have always had a soft spot for Daisy, my first calf love.

How well I can recall those childhood days at home and the innocent fun we used to have. The evenings gathered around the piano, my mother playing and singing, and all of us having to do our turn as best we could. There was no radio or television in those days, yet we enjoyed ourselves immensely. I think perhaps more than the sophisticated youngsters of today with all their electronic entertainment with blaring music and song.

In 1919, after the war was over, things changed somewhat in the grammar school. Some of the lady teachers and older male temporary wartime ones left, and their places were taken by masters who had been officers in the army. Our new headmaster was Major Lloyd Morgan. He was a very fine man, who had unfortunately lost a leg in the war and had an artificial one. He was a good disciplinarian but fair and liked by everyone. The only occasion that I was sent up to his study to be disciplined was by a sports master over an incident during a practice football game one afternoon. We were two practice sides playing each other; the sports master was playing on the opposing side to me and was also refereeing the game. He was using his weight quite a lot, knocking our side off the ball. Quite fairly, I being quite a sizable lad around five foot nine and weighing around one hundred and fifty pounds, decided to play his game and knocked him off the ball once or twice. He did not like it and threatened to strike me; he was our boxing instructor as well. In the heat of the moment I stood up to him and said 'go ahead, hit me'; he did not but ordered me off the field. At first I would not leave the field as I thought I was being treated unfairly. I was one of the first eleven at the time and loved my game and had never been ordered off the field before. He threatened to stop the game altogether if I did not leave, so I left. He duly reported me to the Head and I was summoned to the study, fully expecting to receive 'six of the best'. After listening to my side of it, he gave me a lecture on discipline and to do what I was told to do, even if I thought it was unjust. Instead of the 'six of the best', my punishment was that I was suspended from our next match against a neighbouring school.

This, I think, I felt more than I would have from six across the rear. To my chagrin we lost the match, the only one we lost that season. I do not suppose my playing would have made any difference to the result though.

Haverfordwest
Grammar
School 1st
Eleven Soccer
Team, 1920-21.[1]

The last two years I played for the first elevens in football and cricket, and remember making thirty-nine not out in my last game for the school. I was also elected captain of the 'County Boys'. I was, of course, very honoured to be captain of the County Boys in my last year or so, particularly as I did not excel at any of the athletics, but I suppose I was a fair all-rounder. In athletics, cross-country was my favourite and best event; though I never won it, my best was second. This was a gruelling event and was usually won by one of the country boys. Maybe we had more stamina than the town boys and the boarders. But they usually beat us in the shorter distance events. I was no sprinter but I could keep going. These were very happy days which I thoroughly enjoyed.

As well as the headmaster, there were four other ex-army officers amongst the new masters. I think they found it difficult and boring settling down to teaching after four years' fighting. One of these, Mr George Phillips had lost an arm; he was a local man who ended the war with the rank of captain. He was our Latin master and often used to become exasperated with us, and I do not blame him as I look back. We must have been rather a dumb lot, at least in Latin, as I remember being top in one of our terminal exams with a mark of 41 per cent. George and I are still good friends and we often have a drink together and laugh over those days.

Somehow or other I seemed to keep out of trouble in school, having escaped the birch, and I can only remember being involved in one fight. This was in my first year in the fourth, against a form mate of mine named James, who sat next to me. I do not recollect what it was about, probably nothing much, and we were probably egged on by some of the other boys. But down to the fives court we went at lunchtime, as this was the recognised arena. I do not think either of us was a winner, but James had a beautiful black eye the next Monday when he appeared in school, whilst I had nothing to show for it. I never liked quarrelling or fighting and it used to upset me. However, I could enjoy a friendly boxing bout in the ring with the gloves on.

My schooldays were about over. My Uncle Harry had been asked to try and place me as an apprentice to a shipping company, and a few days before I was to sit my Senior Central Welsh Board Examination, which was the equivalent to the present-day 'O' level exams *(since replaced by the GCSE)*, I went to Cardiff to sign my indentures. I had already bought my uniform. Thus ended my schooldays. I often wonder how I would have done in that examination; as I was joint top of the form in this final year, I kid myself that I would have been successful and passed it.

CHAPTER 2

HEAVE HO AND AWAY
TO SEA WE GO

As far back as I can remember it was always my desire to go to sea, become captain of a large passenger liner and see the world. In those days it was the only way to see the world. Maybe the sea was in my blood, as my mother's father *Capt. Henry Williams, b. 1840* was a sailing ship captain; three of her four brothers went to sea in sail and became master mariners *(Jack, James and Henry)*. I had read all the books I could get hold of written about the sea. How they used to thrill me. I imagined walking the spotless wooden decks and all the adventure that went with going to sea in those days. I was soon to be sadly disillusioned.

It was 13 June 1921 when I received the letter from my uncle asking me to come up to Cardiff on 19 June for an interview with a shipping company, with a view to signing Apprentice Indentures. Mother was worried about her boy leaving home for the first time, *(he was 15 years and 10 months old)* but I was agog with excitement at the thought that at last I might be starting my sea-going career. I was soon busy getting my things together. I had been given a list of clothes, etc. that I would need; amongst other things I had to bring my own bed mattress and bed clothes. Mother insisted I take a feather bed as I had always been used to sleeping on one. My uniform I had had made six months previously, ready for this day; now the day was near when I could wear it. I had tried it on many times in the house and admired it, looking at myself in the mirror, imagining the gold braid on my sleeves and hat which I hoped to be able to wear some day.

The next day at school I informed the Headmaster that this week would be my last in school and that I would not be able to sit the Examination the following week. I was sorry in a way that I could not take the Examination, but instead I would be getting launched on my sea-going career. That weekend I said goodbye to my pals and told them the exciting news.

On Monday 19 June, I was awake early that morning and everything was hustle and bustle. The pony had to be brought in from the field, groomed and harnessed, and my things loaded into the governors' car. It was not long before we were on our way to the railway station to catch the mid-morning train. Train journeys were always exciting in those days, but to me, today was even more so, as I did not know when I should be returning, and when I did, I would have seen some of the foreign lands that I had read so much about. In these days the aeroplane was only in its experimental stage and was not being used as a means of transport. The only way to see the world was by ship. Mother and dad drove me to the station, where I first said goodbye to 'Prince' our pony who I was so fond of. We then went on to the platform to await our train. We had arrived well in advance of the train departure time and patiently waited for it. Eventually the signal arm dropped and we heard the shrill whistle as it approached the bend just before the station, then it appeared round the bend.

It was quite a wrench saying goodbye to mother and dad, not knowing when I would see them again. My baggage and I were bundled into the train, the guard's whistle sounded and the train started to slowly move out. My new life was starting. I frantically waved goodbye from the window until we turned the bend and then I felt alone, very alone; my sixteenth birthday was still two months away. There was one consolation that my uncle would be at Cardiff station to meet me and I was very fond of him. I found it very difficult to settle down in the train and spent most of the journey looking at the passing countryside and the different people at the stations. The journey seemed endless but eventually we arrived.

Then came that milestone in my life when, on 20 June, I signed my Apprentice Indentures[1] with J.C. Gould Steamship Co. Ltd of Cardiff.[2] I was greatly excited as I went down to Cardiff Docks to join my ship and put my foot on the first rung of the ladder I hoped to climb; it actually happened that I had to climb up a rung ladder to get aboard rather than use a gangplank. The name of the ship was the *Grelgrant (4,785 tons)*. In the distance she looked very large and fine. She was berthed under one of the coal tips but they were not working due to the national coal strike that was in progress. It was with some trepidation that I climbed the ladder in my nice new uniform with my kit-bag on my back. Everywhere there was coal dust. I was somewhat taken aback as I reached the top of the ladder, stepped on deck and looked around. Instead of the clean wooden decks I stepped onto a steel deck thickly covered in coal dust; the white paintwork was also thick with it; there was coal dust everywhere.

I was taken to the mate, a big burly man over six foot tall and weighing about 220 pounds, with a squint in his eye. He looked rather terrifying to me and I wished I was back at home with mum on the farm. Although he had a rough and gruff exterior, he later turned out to be, underneath it all, a very kind hearted man who I liked and respected – though one had to be a little wary of him when the moon was full!

Offices of J.C. Gould Bros on James Street, Cardiff, *c.*1910. (CLC)

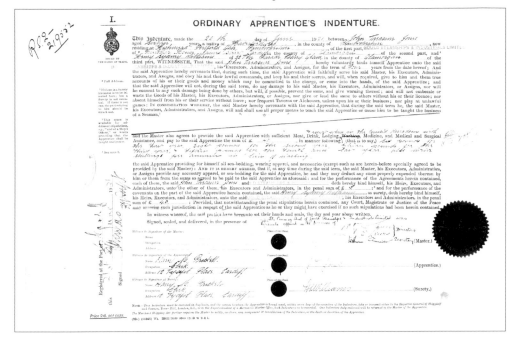

Apprentice's Indenture – signed on.

I was soon told to get out of my uniform and that I would only want that to impress the girls when I went ashore. The uniform of the day and everyday was dungarees – jeans, as they are now called. The next shock I received was when I was shown the quarters which was to be my home for the next four years. It consisted of one room about 15ft long and 9ft wide with six wooden bunks, one settee, one small cupboard or wardrobe, a chest of drawers with six drawers. In the centre was a wooden table to eat and write on and a wooden form for seating. By the door was a handbasin and a free-standing coal stove with a metal uptake through the deck-head to take away the smoke and fumes. This was the home for us six apprentices. The room had almost as much coal dust in it as the deck outside. It was very dirty, and no wonder as this was the only space we had to live, eat, sleep, wash and clean ourselves. The only facilities for ablutions were the one small washbasin and some buckets. The water available was cold water from the hand pump out on deck or walking down to the engine room and asking the engineer-on-watch if we could have some of his hot water from the condensers when it was available at sea. If he was in a good mood he would let us have some, otherwise he would tell us to get the hell out of it. The same applied when it came to washing our clothes. The only way we could bathe ourselves was from a bucket, either in the cabin or, if the weather was not too cold, on the open deck. We always had to make sure we bought enough soap to last us from one port to another. The only thing we could buy on-board was cigarettes and tobacco which the captain used to stock and sell to the crew. I was the only first-trip apprentice on board, the other five having been to sea between six months and two years. In their different ways they were all a grand lot of chaps. But, without exception, they all advised me not to unpack my bag but, to get back on the train, and to go back home to the farm.

My first job was to go down to the holds and help clean them out as there had been coal in them. This was, I am sure, worse than being down the coal mine as far as the dust went. The dust got everywhere – in our lungs, eyes and ears. It was most difficult to clean ourselves properly afterwards with just a bucket to bath in. For hours afterwards I would be coughing up coal dust from my lungs and chest.

In a few days' time we sailed and the adventure, such as it was, started for me. At last I was off to sea. The ship, having no cargo in her, was very light out of the water and rolled for the least little sea and swell. What with this and the coal dust, it was not long before I was looking and feeling as green as the sea and was soon very seasick. Sick or not, I had to continue working as best I could. Work meant twelve hours a day; physical work from 7 a.m. until 6 p.m., then steering the ship or keeping lookout during the night hours, as we were on 'watch and watch'. This meant four hours on duty and four hours off, during the whole twenty-four hours. The Boatswain, who we worked under, suggested a good cure for seasickness was to drink some salt water; I, being very much a greenhorn then, believed him and drank some. You can imagine the result – I was even sicker than before. On top of this I was very homesick and, believe me, if I could have walked off the ship, then I would have done so and the sea would never have seen me again. I even wrote home from the first port and asked my parents to get me out of it at the end of the voyage. However, I overcame the seasickness and homesickness; besides, I felt I could never face my school friends if I went home, so before the voyage ended I decided I would stick it out. I have never regretted this decision even though my sea-going life has had its ups and downs, and I don't mean just the pitching of the ship.

The first sight of a foreign land was a great thrill for me. This was the Island of Fayal in the Azores where we called to refuel with coal. It was a beautiful sunny Sunday morning when the islands showed up and as we approached the harbour to anchor I can still see the gaily coloured and clean looking houses in the distance with the green and brown around them, the morning sun showing it all up to advantage. After seeing nothing but sea for about a week, it looked like paradise to me. Then there were the local vendors coming off in their brightly coloured boats and local costume, with their local wares for sale, as well as the 'bum-boat' men with their soap and matches, etc. Life seemed worth living again, and from this moment I began to take a new lease of life. The sea did not seem so bad after all and maybe there was adventure ahead.

The *Grelgrant* was not the fastest of tramp steamers *(tramp-steamers carried cargo over non-regular routes)*. In fact, I think she must have been the slowest on the oceans, as I cannot recall us ever overtaking another ship, unless it was stopped and broken down. I know it took us twenty-one days from Cardiff to Norfolk, Virginia. A good day's run was 180 miles *equivalent to 7.5 knots* and that only when the seas were smooth.

This was my first sight of America and the New World of which I had read so much. In my youth the Buffalo Bill stories were my favourites; these we used to buy for three pennies or less. We were unable to go ashore at Norfolk but I remember enjoying sitting on deck in the sun, fishing, in my off-duty hours. We remained at anchor in here for two weeks before we received orders to proceed to Galveston to load a cargo of bulk grain. By this time all the coal dust had been cleared away and the ship was at last nice and clean, and we had more amenable work to do.

Galveston holds many impressionable memories for me – some good and some not so good. The not so good ones were the heat, the mosquitoes and the grain dust. On board the ship was so hot, we could not get cool; even at nights we just lay in our bunks with no clothes and were in a bath of perspiration, whilst at the same time it seemed we were being eaten alive by the mosquitoes. They seemed to particularly like my young blood and the change of diet, as I was a mass of bites. These were the 'real Texas mosquitoes' – big fellas, with big bites. It was necessary to keep the portholes closed when loading the grain or we should have been stifled with grain dust; for those who have not experienced this, I can assure you coal dust was preferable. The majority of our cargoes were coal out and grain home, so in port we lived in, and either breathed coal or grain dust.

The pleasant memories were firstly that Galveston was the first place I set foot on American soil and the soil of any foreign country. I was glad that it should have been America. Secondly, was bathing in lovely warm waters of the gulf, under the moonlight. How beautifully warm the water was after the cool water around Britain. Thirdly, was tasting water melon for the first time; in fact I had never even seen one before. I bought the biggest one I could find; it was huge, and all for 5 cents. I loved them, and what a change to the diet of salt beef, salt pork and salt fish, which was our staple diet at sea. If we were lucky we had an egg once a week on Sundays for breakfast. Our milk ration was one 16 ounce tin of condensed milk for three weeks. This we were forced to share with the cockroaches with which the ship and our cabin were infested. Still, we became used to it all and remained healthy and strong; I cannot recall any of us being ill. In spite of all this we were a happy little gang, and in the nice warm evenings at sea we would sit out on the hatches, playing an assortment of musical instruments and having a sing-song.

Having returned to the UK and off-loaded the cargo of grain, we returned to our home port of Cardiff. There were plenty of pubs around the shipping office and they used to do a roaring trade, especially when a ship paid off and not too badly when one signed on, as most of the crew were given an advance note for a couple of pounds. These, the boarding house keepers and local traders would cash for a commission. They always took a certain degree of risk when they did so as they were not cashable at the ship owner's office until the ship had sailed and if the man failed to join, they would not be honoured; hence the fact that they charged quite a high commission for cashing them. Often these notes proved worthless as some of the men would get rotten drunk and miss their ship. As well as being given an advance note the men had the option of taking out an allotment note to leave a percentage of their pay to their wives, etc. These were paid fortnightly or monthly as desired. If a man deserted his ship, the first thing the captain did was to inform the Owners so that the allotment note could be stopped.

The loading took three days and three nights. During this time there was not much we could do in the way of work except odd jobs and help shift the ship sometimes and load the stores on board.

The crew were ordered aboard for midnight. The last truck of coal was tipped around 2 a.m. and the trimmers were trimming the last of it down so we could put the hatches on and batten

Roath Dock Cardiff, *c.*1920. (© National Museum of Wales)

down the holds. We all turned to at 4 a.m. to secure the ship for sea as the tide was at 6 a.m. and we would start leaving the berth at 5 a.m. Many of the sailors had imbibed quite a lot of liquor and had not had time to sleep it off. In due course we found ourselves once more out in the Bristol Channel steaming slowly seaward. There was one advantage of employing Arab[3] firemen *(presumed to be stokers, who fired the boilers)*, as they did not drink and therefore were usually fit on sailing to do their job efficiently. This could not always be said of a white crew in these days, particularly if we sailed in the evenings or early morning.

This voyage we were bound for the East to discharge our coal at Perim at the south end of the Red Sea. This meant going through the Mediterranean Sea and the Suez Canal. This is one of the interesting things about tramping; we never knew where we were going to next. At this time we did not know where we would go to from Perim. It would doubtless be somewhere in the East where we would load our next cargo. The other boys took great pleasure in telling me all about the canal and all the odd Arab characters I would meet there with their pseudo Scottish names. How they would swarm aboard with their wares, dirty postcards, etc. and the little 'gilly gilly' boys who would produce live baby chicks from almost anywhere. Also, what expert pickpockets the little rascals were and that they would steal anything if given the slightest chance. They told me of the terrible name the Red Sea had for heat. How unbearable it could be in the worst parts and that Perim was reputed to be one of the hottest places there.

On this journey we had plenty of company, very different to the lonely previous one crossing the Atlantic when we rarely saw a ship. This is probably one of the busiest routes in the world. We rounded Longships, the lighthouse off the south-western extremity of the English mainland, and then headed across the dreaded Bay of Biscay for Cape Finisterre, the north-western point of the Spanish mainland. Fortunately for me, the Bay was on its best behaviour this time, there being little wind and the sea smooth, otherwise I would no doubt have succumbed once more to *Mal de Mere*.

The mate found a nice dirty job for us again. Down the holds once more, on top of the coal this time, scaling the deckheads and the ship's side that was not covered by the coal. This was even dirtier than sweeping the holds, though it was not quite so dusty. The rust and dust we scaled off got into our hair, eyes and ears. To try and keep some of it out of our hair we covered our hair with cap covers. To make matters worse the sun beating down on the steel decks, especially in the intense heat of the Red Sea made it almost unbearable. As fast as we drank water to quench our thirsts we sweated it out again. What a joy it was to leave the hold to take one's turn at the wheel. It was like leaving hell and going up to heaven for a little while, enjoying the clean fresh air under the canvas awning, which kept the glaring sun off the wooden bridge deck under which the captain lived. It also kept it off the mate and myself; however, I think that protecting the deck was more important than keeping the sun off the mate and me.

The first mate kept the four to eight watches, the second mate the twelve to four watches and the third mate the eight to twelve.

00.00 to 04.00 hrs: second mate	*12.00 to 16.00 hrs: second mate*
04.00 to 08.00 hrs: first mate	*16.00 to 20.00 hrs: first mate*
08.00 to 12.00 hrs: third mate	*20.00 to 24.00 hrs: third mate*

Whilst on the bridge the second and third mates were invariably sewing canvas, making tarpaulins, boat and ventilator covers. There was nothing romantic about the work that I had been given to do so far. I liked steering the ship in daytime but not much at night as I found so much difficulty in keeping awake. At night we much preferred to be on lookout, or better still, on the standby in our rooms or in the galley. It was a thousand miles to Gibraltar and close on three *(thousand)* to Port Said; this would take us fifteen days. There was much to see on this passage so the time passed fairly quickly. Cape St Vincent was the focal turning point off the south-western corner of Portugal for vessels entering and coming from the Mediterranean, unless they were heading for the west coast of Africa.

I saw ships of all sorts, shapes and sizes. I was lucky enough to see the *Kaisar I Hind (see colour section No.1)*, one of the very fine P&O passenger ships. She was a magnificent sight as she sped past us, homeward bound, looking like a sleek greyhound with the white feather at her stem, while her white bow-wave, black hull and funnels and buff upper-works; astern of her one could see her wake stretching for miles. I was at the wheel at the time so had a good view as she passed about a mile away. My attention wandered from the compass as I imagined myself on the bridge as her captain. I was abruptly brought back to reality by a roar from the mate 'where the hell do you think you are going'. I quickly looked at the compass to find I was fifteen degrees off course and still swinging the wrong way. I thought 'my god, I will never become a captain if I do not pay more attention to what I am doing' and quickly brought the ship back to her course. From then on I kept my eye on the compass, whilst the mate kept his eye on me and the wake.

One of the greatest difficulties we young apprentices had was to keep awake at night whilst on lookout or steering the ship. This was especially so in the warm tropics. I often found it physically impossible to do so as we never had more than 3½ hours' sleep at a stretch. Many a time I have fallen asleep walking on lookout and only wakened when my knees gave way under me. Many a time the officer on watch found me with my eyes closed at the wheel and the ship going off course. For this I was sometimes punished by having to stay an extra half an hour of my watch below taking the wheel, thus missing some more of my sleep.

Left: Kaiser-I-Hind.

Below: BP Tanker, *c.*1921. (JCM)

The next day we entered the Straits of Gibraltar; the east-going current pushed up our speed to eleven knots, a fantastic speed for us. We glided past Tarifa Lighthouse with the high, barren-looking hills behind it and soon the Rock of Gibraltar started to appear in sight on the port bow. Ships were now passing us very close on both sides, so I had to keep a very careful watch on my steering. This gave me a real thrill and I felt proud that I was allowed to steer through here. As we came closer to the Rock I could see many ships at anchor in the bay and the masts and funnels of some of our big warships in the harbour. The Rock did not appear as imposing to me as I had expected it to, but, as we passed two miles south of it I could see how impregnable it looked. I was intrigued by the large sloping concrete surfaces on the eastern side of the Rock until Alf told me that it was a catchment area made to collect the water when it rained; this was then stored in reservoirs inside the Rock. Many years later I was to come to know the Rock well, but now everything was new, strange and fascinating to me.

Whilst steaming through the Mediterranean one of the things that impressed me most was the steady stream of oil tankers that we passed, most of which belonged to the same company, the British Petroleum Company. Those westbound were deep in the water and those eastbound very light in ballast. They were all faster than we were and probably did twelve knots. They had quite distinctive funnel markings and their names all started with 'British'. They always looked spotlessly clean.

Life had now settled down into a routine of work, eat, and sleep. The only exception to this was in the dog watches in the evening, between four and eight; this could be called our social period. We chatted, played our musical instruments, sang along without someone yelling 'shut up, I am trying to sleep'. Some of us got together learning some navigation from our books and testing each other on our seamanship and rules of the road. To be able to pass our examinations we had to learn off, word perfect, the whole of the Thirty-one Articles.

Ten days after we passed through the Straits of Gibraltar we arrived at Port Said. This was the 'Gateway to the East' as all ships passed through the Canal to get there. On average ships took about twelve hours to pass through the ninety-odd miles, many took longer. The ships one way had to tie up to the banks whilst the others passed, unless they happened to meet in the Bitter Lakes where there was room to pass without tying up. This was usually decided by the stations ashore and depended on the flow of the current and the amount of ships in each direction.

Having to tie up was most unpopular with us as it meant, if you were unlucky, you spent a lot of your watch on stations tying your ship up and watching the mooring as others steamed very slowly by. If you were really unlucky you could end up being on duty for twelve hours and then only having four hours off.

There is no other place in the world like Port Said. It had a character and characters all of its own. I do not think there was a sailor who did not like the jovial rascals like Jock McPherson and Sandy MacKay, Arabs who had given themselves Scottish names and were known the world over. They were likable fellows and we had much fun haggling with them over the price of their wares, even if we did not intend buying anything. They always started with some outrageous price and would eventually sell for about quarter of it, if you haggled long enough. Basically I think that they were reasonably honest, though there were plenty of pick-pockets and thieves around.

I was told that ashore here every vice was practiced, but I did not venture ashore to test the truth of this. Many touts came along and whispered in your ear 'you want nice girl, twelve, or nice young boy or dirty postcards'.

Most ships used Port Said as a bunkering port, it being a sort of halfway stage and the price was probably better here than further east. Large stockpiles were kept here for this purpose. This was probably the busiest bunkering port in the world. The coal came off in barges or lighters. Large wooden planks or gangways would be rigged from the lighters to the ship and a continuous stream of Arabs ran up and down these carrying the coal in small baskets, either on their heads or shoulders. They formed a human chain. They were a sorry sight, with

Port Said – coaling from lighters 1. (© National Maritime Museum, London)

Port Said – coaling from lighters 2. (© National Maritime Museum, London)

young boys and old men clothed in rags. They were, I believe, paid so much for each basket they loaded and that it was a mere pittance. They lived in compounds on the east side of the canal. I could not believe it possible that people could live and work like that. It almost made me sick; I felt terribly sorry for them; what an existence. I thought our conditions were bad enough, but seeing them made me feel as if I was living like a Rajah.

Before we could enter the canal we had to take a searchlight aboard and a crew from the canal company. The searchlight was contained in a large square box which we had to rig over the stern. This was to light up the buoys and the banks of the canal during the dark so the pilot could navigate safely. There seemed to be a continual stream of traffic coming and going through here. This place fascinated me, my first sight of the Arab world.

The bunkering had finished and we were turned-to to clean up the decks and put the sweeping into the bunkers – nothing was wasted in these ships – and then gave the decks a quick wash down to get rid of the worst of the dust.

The chief engineer had checked and signed for his coal and the captain had just returned from ashore with the Agent. It was my watch on deck and at 10 p.m. the Canal Pilot boarded and said we would be sailing in half an hour. It was my wheel from 10 p.m. to 12 a.m. so I would have the job of steering through the first part of the canal. At 10.30p.m. we let go the lines and with the aid of the tugs we turned and headed for the entrance of the canal.

I was quite thrilled at the idea of steering in the canal as, by now, I was pretty good at it, provided I could keep awake. As we approached the entrance, the searchlight was switched on and we were soon steering slowly in the canal. It was not difficult to steer here and the Pilot kept slightly adjusting the course to steer. We were now steering by the buoys in the canal and midway between the banks; if the ship came a bit closer to one side than the other, she was apt to take a sheer into the bank. After a few miles we had left Port Said and most of the buildings behind and were now proceeding quietly and smoothly through the desert. It seemed very strange to me to be going along through this narrow channel of water with desert sands on both sides of us; it was eerie but exciting. The only sounds were the occasional car on the road which ran alongside the canal on the west side and the odd Arab who gave us a shout from the bank as we passed. Many of these could be seen sleeping, wrapped up in their blankets, up on the banks. Once the sun had gone the temperature rapidly dropped and it became quite cold. About an hour after leaving Port Said we came to El Kantara. Here, there was a ferry across as it was a British army base, and, though it was now near midnight, many British soldiers could be seen around. Midnight came and my watch ended. It had been an interesting day, but I was now very tired and ready for bed and was soon asleep.

But alas I was not to have an undisturbed watch below. At 3 a.m. we were all called as we had to tie up to the bank to let a northbound convoy of ships through; this did not please me. The ship was stopped and the Arab boat put over the side, their job was to take our mooring lines ashore and make them fast to the post ashore so we could heave ourselves alongside the bank. This was simple enough a task as there was no wind. In the distance we could see the mast-head lights of the first ship coming along. I was stationed on the forecastle head with the mate, so could see the ships as they came along. The first ship was a deeply laden British tanker who came by so slowly she hardly seemed to be moving. As she approached less than a ship's length away, our ship started to move about. This was due to the water that was being pushed ahead of the tanker. As she passed we seemed to be sucked out towards her and the ropes had to be carefully tended or they would have parted and we might have swung out and collided with the passing ship. It was therefore necessary to have good mooring lines and for ships to pass as slowly as possible.

We remained there whilst six ships passed and each time we had to carefully watch our lines and the Pilot and the captain helped with the engines to keep us in position. This was a long operation which lasted two hours. It was to start with most interesting to me to see these other ships pass so close and everyone that passed gave a wave and the odd shout. We were all glad when the last ship passed and we were under way again; by now it was well into my watch on deck. I did not have a wheel this watch for which I was thankful as I doubt whether I could have kept awake just staring at the compass or concentrating on the canal ahead.

This was the only time we had to stop and tie up. I think we were four ships in our group and we passed another convoy of ships in the Bitter Lakes. During the day the sun beat down and it became really hot again.

We arrived at Suez, the southern end of the canal, about 2 p.m., discharged our Pilot, put off the Arabs and their boats, and landed the searchlight into a tender. Then we were off down the Gulf of Suez heading for the Red Sea.

The next few weeks I was to find out what really hot weather was like; though it had been very hot in Galveston that was to prove nothing to what we were to experience. In the Red Sea it usually blows from the north. Thus, when proceeding south, there appears to be no breeze at all, with the smoke going straight up; this is known as 'Paddy Hurricane'. Though we sweltered on deck and in our cabins it was nothing to what the poor stokers had to contend with in the stokeholds, shovelling coal onto the fires, raking them and cleaning out the ashes. It must have been pure hell for them. They used to appear on deck almost prostrate with heat exhaustion, sit there for a while and recover, then back down below. They used to be given lots of oatmeal water and lime juice to help keep them going. The steam used to fall away badly at times and seldom did the safety valve lift and blow off steam. We slept on deck under old tarpaulins stretched over the derricks to keep the sun off in the day and the night dampness and dew at night. Here it was stinking hot, day and night.

At last we reached our port of discharge, Perim.[4] What a hole this turned out to be. It was purely a bunkering station with a couple of whites running it and some Arab labour. It was a hellhole to live in and for years on end it must have been almost unbearable, yet Britishers used to do it. Even in this heat and sun we were put over the side to scale the rust and red lead it. We were soon as brown as the Arabs. At night time the dynamo was shut down and we had to use paraffin lamps for light; this made the place hotter than ever. Hell would have had difficulty in beating this place, and on top of it all, the infernal coal dust.

We existed here for ten days and with great sighs of relief we finished discharging. The captain had received orders to proceed to Fremantle,[5] Western Australia, for orders, so we headed south and out into the Gulf of Aden. This was a long trek to Australia, a matter of just over five thousand miles. This would take us around twenty seven days. This was four weeks of deadly routine watch-keeping, cleaning the holds, rigging shifting boards for grain, scaling and painting, eating and sleeping. However the weather was a great improvement on that of the Red Sea and Perim. I settled down to studying in the dog watches and on my stand-bys and was now starting to show a little progress on my Articles, and beginning to be able to do some of the simpler navigation from the books.

At last Australia was getting nearer and the captain received orders to proceed to Geraldton, a small port about two hundred miles north of Fremantle. This was a day nearer than Fremantle and on the twenty-seventh day after leaving Perim we sighted the Australian coast. My recollections of it were that it was fairly low-lying, with hills in the background. However, I can picture the rickety wooden wharf we tied up to, which protruded well out from the shore and down which we had to walk to the very small little town, if it could be called that in those days. It was more a village with a few stores and I doubt if the population could have been more than one thousand at that time. I recollect this place so well as it was where I spent my first Christmas away from home. I was now sixteen. It was to be the most inhospitable port I ever visited. Maybe they were not used to sailors and lived a secluded life there. I cannot remember talking to anyone other than to the men who loaded the ship. One of their pet phrases was 'good morning you f★★king bastard'; this seemed to be a friendly greeting. Christmas Eve I recall walking up the one street in the town; there did not seem to be a soul around, but there was music coming from some of the houses, some of which was carols and some favourites of ours at home. I felt terribly homesick and almost wept and returned to the ship. This was my first impression of Australia and I was not impressed. The grain we loaded here was all in bags, brought along on a small railway alongside the ship. The stevedores rigged chutes into the holds down which the bags were diverted to various parts of the hold, thus saving a great deal of labour in carrying the bags. It took about two weeks to load there and then we were off again – this time to discharge in Marseilles.

Marseilles seemed to bring a sparkle into all the sailors' eyes. It became a conversation piece amongst the apprentices, some of whom had visited French ports before and had recounted to me some of their experiences at some of them. Women and girls were quite often the topic of conversation amongst seafarers and after four weeks at sea it was a treat just to see a girl in the distance, dressed up in pretty clothes. I listened to many stories told by the others of visits to the red-light districts and what they saw, and what could and did happen. I was slowly being put wise to the pit-falls of the unwary sailor and, for the first time, heard about venereal disease and the horrors of it; the risks men ran if they associated with these women and the precautions they must take if they did. It was most unusual, apparently, in those days after visiting a port, not to have one or two sailors or firemen reporting to the chief steward a week or so later that they had trouble. In those days there was little that could be done at sea to help them and they were put ashore at the first opportunity for treatment. I was very ignorant of these things at that time, but I was learning fast.

In due course, we arrived at Marseille to discharge our cargo. We all had a small 'sub' from the captain and off we went ashore to see some of the sights of the port. This was my first visit to a French port. In those days licensed prostitution was legal and I understood from the others that there were streets of these houses. After walking around for a while we went into one of the street cafes for a beer. It was not long before one or two girls sidled up to our table and asked us to buy them a drink. We had very little money but one of the boys bought them a drink. It was not long before they were making suggestions to us to go home with them. We did not go along with these proposals and after we joked with them and finished our beer we left, strolled around for a while and returned to the ship. My eyes were being opened.

When we arrived back at Cardiff I was allowed to go home on a few days' leave. What a joy it was to see mother and my brothers and sister again. Although I wrote regularly to mother, I had to relate my experiences and tell them what an apprentice's life was like and the foreign lands I had visited.

I was now somewhat a man of the world. Soon after I went to sea my father bought a very nice farm of one hundred and ten acres about half a mile outside the outskirts of Haverfordwest *(Slade Hall on the Portfield Road)*. They had moved there whilst I was away, so I did not return to my childhood home and have never been in the house since. I was thrilled with the new house we had, but again there was no bathroom or hot and cold running water; some years later my mother had this remedied. When I had left home my youngest sister was only nineteen months old; she was now running about and starting to talk. I was very loath to leave to rejoin the ship when my time was up.

My next voyage took me to Buenos Aires. This was a long passage of around six thousand miles and took us about forty days. Once we were clear of the Bay of Biscay the weather was warm and pleasant, and even in the tropics it never approached the terrible heat of the Red Sea. In fact it is one of the most pleasant runs I know and there was always plenty of company around. It was a tricky passage for the captain, up between the various sand banks in the Rio de la Plata estuary, but we eventually moored up safely at the Boca, the coal discharging harbour.

Buenos Aires was one of the ports I was to visit more than any other foreign port during my time in tramp steamers, and one I came to like very much. This, I think, had the most popular 'Mission to Seamen' in the world, at least amongst apprentices and it certainly was as far as I was concerned. It had a special apprentices' room and no-one else was allowed in there. The mission was in the charge of Canon Brady,[6] very ably assisted by the Revd Law. Two very fine and popular men.

Above left: Revd Canon H.W. Brady, OBE, BA. (MTS)

Above right: Canon Brady and his flock. (MTS)

The Mission to Seamen *(now known as The Mission to Seafarers),*[7] a fine Christian organisation, is run for the benefit of the seamen, to help look after their morals and welfare in the ports all over the world. They have done, and still do, fine work on our behalf and we seamen are most grateful to them and all those who assist the Missions. They were homes from homes, especially for us apprentices and the young seamen.[8]

Around this area were some of the lowest 'dives' in South America. Here prostitution was not illegal and, I believe, the incidence of VD was high. We had not been tied up long before Canon Brady paid a visit to the ship, told of the evils of the city and invited us all to come up to the Mission Hall each evening or anytime we were off duty. I think all of us, except the one who was on night duty, went to the Mission that evening and met many apprentices from other ships in the harbour and some of the young ladies who visited the Mission to help entertain us. They were a fine lot of girls. The senior girl was Lola Woods, a little thing, probably in her mid-twenties, full of life and cheer. For years every apprentice who ever sailed to Buenos Aires knew Lola. I think she spent at least half of the evenings of the week at the Mission. There were about half-a-dozen of these charming girls who came there to help make life more pleasant for us apprentices. They were mostly daughters of English people who held positions in and around the city. Another I remember well and sometimes had the pleasure of seeing home was Maud Mortimer; her father was chief engineer of the big meat factory down the docks and they lived nearby where we docked. These girls were not permitted to go home alone.

We had about five weeks here discharging and loading. Each night I spent at the Mission, it was a real home from home. On Friday nights there was always boxing at the Mission.[9] Canon Brady was a keen boxer and so, I believe, was Revd Law. This was a very popular night. I was fond of boxing myself. One of these evenings there was a second cook from one of the regular traders offering to box anyone around his own weight, but no one would take him on. This went against my Welsh blood and I offered to take him on. I think the other boys thought I was a fool and in for a hiding, as he seemed to be known there. The fight was always three, two minute rounds. I realised I was up against someone good and might get a hiding; I may have been a fool but no one ever frightened me and I always loved a challenge. We had a jolly good scrap and came out about even. From that day on, whenever I visited Buenos Aires, the Canon always had me boxing. Alf, our senior apprentice, rather fancied his chances and we two had three rounds one Friday evening. We had been invited out to Lola Woods' home afterwards to meet her mother and have some supper. I'm afraid we went out somewhat dishevelled and Alf had a couple of black eyes. He only mentioned this to me quite recently when I met him for the first time after forty-seven years. I had many interesting bouts there at various times, always with someone from a ship. The last one I had was when I was about nineteen. This time Canon Brady wanted me to have three rounds with an Argentine bank clerk. I had not fought foreigners before, many of the Argentineans were very good fighters, and I was not at all keen to do so. Anyhow, Canon Brady prevailed on me and I said I would, just for an exhibition round. He was around my own size and weight and I weighed him up from my corner. The bell went and he rushed out of his corner and came for me with everything he had. It was obvious he was not treating it as an exhibition, so I had no option but to make a fight of it, and fight it was. We were pretty evenly matched but I was determined not to be beaten by an Argentinean in front of my shipmates, so I pulled out all the stops and put all I knew and all my energy into the fight. It was pretty even up to the start of the third round, though I had received a hard blow on top of the head once when I ducked, which shook me up in the second round. In the third I was getting on top and at the end of the round I had him groggy with his hands by his side, but I did not have enough strength left to give him the *coupe de grasse* and thus it ended. This was the toughest fight I had ever had; I was actually sick afterwards from the blow I had received on the top of my head. I decided, there and then, that was the last time I would go into the ring. I did not return to Buenos Aires again during my apprenticeship, so did not have to say no to Canon Brady. He would probably have persuaded me to go in again if I had.[10]

In the autumn of 1922, not long after the end of the Russian Revolution, we made a voyage through the Dardanelles into the Black Sea, then into the Sea of Azov in Russia to load a cargo of grain. We loaded at a little port call Marianopol.[11] There was nothing there. No one seemed to own anything; 'squatters' rights' seemed to be the order of the day and anyone seemed to go into any house. There was no money in circulation as the rouble then was valueless. In any case, there did not seem to be any shops or anything to buy. The best currency then was soap, clothing and the ordinary necessities of life. For a shirt, underwear, clothing of any sort or soap, which was in great demand, the girls would be most obliging. I am afraid that most of the crew, officers and apprentices left there with depleted wardrobes and a low stock of soap – in fact, very 'schooner rigged' as we sailors would say!

Here, it seemed, the women did a great deal of the manual labour. When loading bulk grain, it is, for safety's sake, essential that the grain in the holds is trimmed right tight up to the deckheads and no empty pockets left. This is to prevent the grain running to one side of the ship when she rolled and eventually capsizing. Many grain-laden ships have been lost through this in the old years. This trimming was usually done by male shore labour, but here in Marianopol it was done by women. It was the officers' job to go down the holds to make sure they trimmed the grain to his satisfaction. I have never known the officers spend so much time down the holds as they did here. Some of the women trimming the grain were young and quite attractive. I know the officers used to fill their pockets with tablets of soap when they went down the holds; they were always empty when they came up, but they had a pleased and satisfied look on their faces – *c'est la vie!* The bum-boat men did good business at our next port of call where the crew re-stocked with clothes and soap, etc.

Whilst in the *Grelgrant* we had some very bad weather. One voyage from Algiers, loaded with a cargo of iron ore for Rotterdam, we hit a real snorter going up the Portuguese coast and we rolled violently with all the weight down in the bottom of the ship. One day we only made good twenty miles and the next we almost stood still. But the worst weather in her was homeward-bound across the Atlantic with a cargo of grain. We had a severe gale blowing on our port quarter, with very big seas that frequently broke over us. This particular night I had the ten to midnight wheel. The wheel was on an open bridge, there being no wheelhouse.

About eleven thirty a huge sea loomed up from the port quarter and broke aboard us. It came up on the bridge, tore the canvas screens and even then the officer on watch and I had to hang on and got soaked. It lifted the port jolly-boat, outside the captain's cabin, out of its chocks and crashed it against the bulkhead of the captain's cabin on the deck below the bridge. It smashed the port lifeboat and also the heavy teak door into the officers' accommodation, knocking down the light wooden bulkhead of the mate's cabin and washing him out of his bunk and flooded the saloon. He was the six foot, 220-pounder, and was a little peeved. All hands were called out to try and repair the damage and secure what was left of the boats, board up the door into the side of the mate's quarters and bail out. I did not come off watch at midnight, in fact it was almost 2 a.m. before I was relieved and could go to bed, to try and get a little sleep before coming on duty again at 4 a.m. The next day, fortunately, the wind went down and so did the seas. To add to our troubles the next day our steering gear broke down. The system was made up of direct manual gearing from the bridge to the steam steering engine in the fore part of the long after well-deck. From the engine were a series of heavy chains around sheaves to long thick metal rods, one each side, which moved in guides between the bulwarks and bulwark stanchions on each side. These then joined up with chains over the poop-deck, which were joined to the quadrant fixed to the top of the rudder post.

The metal rod on the port side broke in half and put the steering out of action. Fortunately there was only a fresh wind and a moderately rough sea at the time. We had no spare rod. So we went into hand steering; this we found most difficult and it required four men at a time. So, we rigged up wire tackles from the quadrant to the drum ends of the mooring winch on the poop and were able to keep some sort of course this way. We then set-to to measure the broken rod and cut a length of wire from our four and a half inch insurance wire and spliced metal thimble eyes in each end. It took us all day to do this and get it fitted. We shackled each end to the chains and it worked beautifully. We were very lucky that this did not happen at the height of the storm we had just come through, or I should not be here trying to write this now. I left the *Grelgrant* some two voyages later and joined the *Grelhead*. The wire we had made and put in place of the rod was so good, and obviously must have passed the surveyors, as it was still there and functioning perfectly when I left. I often wondered if and when they replaced it with a new metal rod.

The following voyage we loaded a cargo of coal for Portland, Maine. This meant crossing the North Atlantic once more; not the nicest of oceans to be in during the winter in a deeply laden tramp. When these ships were deeply laden with a full cargo, there was only about 3ft of freeboard. Quite a few tramp ships were lost here over the years in the bad gales. In bad weather it was dangerous to go out on deck, as seas would be coming over everywhere. There was no other means of getting from one part of the ship to the other, than over the open deck. So, when we had to go out on deck to change watch, etc., it was necessary to bide one's time and do so in-between the seas. Often one was knocked off one's feet and soaked; sea-boots and oilskins were an essential part of one's kit in those days.

There was no crow's-nest up the mast, so we kept our lookout on the forecastle head, which is right in the bows of the ship. In bad weather, in head seas, it was not long before the ship was putting her bows under and the seas came over the lookout position. Before this happened, the officer on watch would call us off there and put us on the bridge to keep our lookout. One dark night, I was on look out on the forecastle head. There was a fresh wind blowing from the west, and the seas were growing bigger and bigger; the ship starting to pitch more and more, sometimes throwing the spray up through the hawser pipes. Further and further she put her bow down to the swell and at times it was almost to the level of the forecastle deck. I was waiting for the mate to call me off to keep my lookout on the bridge, when suddenly she put her nose under and the sea came over the forecastle, knocking me off my feet and I found myself being washed through the rails overboard. I managed to grab the rail and save myself. I did not wait any longer to be called off. I quickly left and reported to the bridge and told the officer what had happened. I am not sure what else I may have said to him but I was not

SS *Grelhead*. (© National Museum of Wales)

very pleased with him keeping me on the forecastle head until I was washed off. I was soaked and somewhat frightened and was sent below to change my clothes.

A few days later we were working coal up out of the cross bunker hatch to have it ready for loading grain the other side. We were working it into the bunker 'tween decks. This meant the beam and one section of hatches was left on and this was used as a working platform to tip the coal into the barrows and wheel it away. (It being hoisted by a rope whip on the winch on the upper deck through the other section of hatches which had been taken off.) In the forenoon I had been working on this section of hatches with the boatswain. During the afternoon, whilst making one of theses hoists, the hook caught in the beam which was supporting and holding the hatches in position, unshipping the beam. The beam, hatches, boatswain and another sailor all plunged into the lower hold amongst the men working down there, resulting in the Boatswain being killed and one of the men suffering a broken pelvis. This was an accident that should never have happened. It appears the Boatswain had forgotten to put bolts in the beam to stop it being unshipped if the hook did catch in it. This was one of the safety precautions that should have been seen to, but had not. This could have been me instead of the boatswain. After that I never worked on hatches without checking that there was a bolt in the beam.

On another occasion, one of the younger apprentices, when putting on the hatches, trod on one which did not fit properly on the beams and he was tipped down into the hold. This was a drop of around thirty feet. To our amazement, he picked himself up and climbed back up the ladder. He had fortunately fallen on the ends of some stacked dunnage wood *(brushwood stowed under or among cargo to prevent wetting and chaffing)* which gave like a spring and eased his fall. He was most fortunate as, more often than not, one would be killed or receive some serious injury; he got away with some bruises and shock. Danger seemed to lurk everywhere; one could not be too careful.

This ended my association with the *Grelgrant*; I was then transferred to the *Grelhead (4,274 tons)* which I joined at Barry. The *Grelhead* was a great improvement accommodation-wise compared to the *Grelgrant*. This was a short well-deck ship and our cabin, though no larger than the previous one, was on its own by the mainmast. We had a bathroom and our own flush toilet. I was sorry to part company with the boys in the *Grelgrant* as they were a grand lot of fellows, but I soon found that the new bunch were also great. In fact they were a very musical lot and we got together a little band, sometimes playing for dances at the Mission we visited. Sinclair could play almost any instrument and had a brass cornet which he played well. The third engineer had a violin which he played reasonably well; we made a drum and cymbals and three of us played mandolins. Most evenings in the nice weather we would sit on the hatches and practice together.

The mate was from my home county and was a teetotaller. He got us all together and lectured us on the evils of drink, telling us that, if he found we had been drinking, he would give us all the dirty jobs for the voyage. I do not know what dirtier tasks he could have found us compared to what I had been doing in the other ship and I fully expected to have to do similar tasks here. We all went ashore that evening to the local *(pub)* and had a few beers and were a little high when we returned. I do not know to this day whether he knew that we had been on the beer that evening. He was an extremely nice man who treated us well and helped us where and when he could; however, he was a glutton for work, but I did not mind working and always took a delight in doing a good day's work, and doing it well. I did not like to think anyone could do a better day's work than I could and used to take pride in doing more than the sailors. This eventually got me into a fight with one of the sailors on the voyage. It was on the way home from India. Amongst our able seamen was one particular fellow who was darn lazy and was also rather a bully and disliked by everyone. He boasted that he had won the Lonsdale Belt at some time. He was in his thirties and I was eighteen at that time.

We had cargo stored in the poop deck. This was exempt from Suez Canal dues provided there was no cargo there, so to avoid paying these dues, we took it out and stored it on the hatch until we were through the canal. After leaving Port Said the mate gave us a job and finish for the day to move this back into the poop; this cargo consisted of two hundred pound sacks of rape seed. There were only about four of us who could carry these bags on our backs and I was one of them. Our lazy sailor was not one of them. We split up into two gangs, one gang working each side, and the bags passed though steel doors into the poop. Two of each side carried the bags to the door and threw them in, whilst the men inside stowed them. We finished our side in good time but they were much slowed on the other side. Our last friend was working that side. We went over to help them, as we couldn't knock off until it was all in. This sailor and another sailor took the bags from our backs. This chap was going very slowly, so I asked him to get a move on as we wished to finish. He thereupon let fly and hit me in the face. Without thinking, I retaliated and he came out to lay about me. The steel deck was like a skating rink with the loose rape seed that had spilled from the bags. Now, I thought, I am in for a hiding. So, always believing attack was the best form of defence, I did not wait for him to hit me again, I lay into him; to my amazement I was getting the better of the exchanges. Then he had me up against the bulwark and came down with both of his clenched fists to strike me on top of the head. I just managed to pull my head back in time and his fists grazed down the front of my face. I saw red and, if I could have, I would have knocked him overboard. I really went for him and landed a few good blows; but we were slipping all over the place and then we both slipped down, with him on top of me. He was attempting to strike me, sitting on top of me, when the others intervened and dragged him off. When I got up he had no further desire to continue the fight, but sat down and cried and started to look for his dentures which I must have knocked out. From that day on he ceased to rule the roost and did not bully anyone. I was a sort of hero and my stock went up. Particularly so with the mate, who had not been able to do much with him, as he was often downright rude to the mates. I disliked quarrels and fights intensely, but if anyone struck me my Welsh blood was up and I was not able to turn the other cheek. This was the first and last fight I ever had at sea, or anywhere else for that matter.

Probationary Midshipman
RNR, with Alf Plummer,
senior apprentice, 1923.

I had now been at sea for two years and nine months. When we came to sail the following voyage, the Boatswain did not join ship, although he had signed on. The captain sent for me and told me he wanted me to take over the Bosun's job. I agreed to, provided he paid me something for doing the job. He agreed, after much humming and hawing, to pay me £2 a month extra to my bit of apprentice pay. This meant I would receive £2 15s (£2.75 *in decimal money*) a month now. This seemed a lot of money to me. I quite liked doing the job and felt very flattered that, after 2½ years at sea, they considered me capable of doing so. I was now the senior apprentice. As Bosun I moved into a two berth cabin which I shared with the carpenter. He was a clean, good living chap who we all liked.

I remained Bosun until the end of my apprenticeship in June 1925. I almost got myself killed on the first voyage as Bosun. Again it was working coal out of the cross bunkers, but this time it was in a very different sort of way. As usual we were short-handed for the job, with the result that we had no one driving the steam winch. We were using a rope whip on the drum-end to hoist the baskets of coal onto the deck and stowing the coal on the upper deck until there was room for it in the side bunker. As Bosun I put myself on the whip. With the first hoist my rope ran foul on the drum end and I stepped across to turn the steam off the winch. As I did so I put my foot in a bight of the rope which was lying on the deck between me and the valve. I was caught by the ankle and flung over the top of the drum end. I went over 'all standing and fast' as the whip drum was turning at high speed with the valve wide open. I was caught by the right ankle with the rope that was winding itself around the drum end. Fortunately, my left leg and body went over the hatch and I landed on the sharp edge of the hatch-coaming, right up to my groin, with my right leg round the drum and jammed there. I could feel my leg being stretched.

One of the sailors flew to the winch and reversed the lever before trying to shut off the valve. The strain came off my leg and I started to go down the hatch, but I was firmly held by the rope. The winch was stopped, but the strain on my leg had almost brought it to a standstill by the time the sailor reached the lever. I really thought my leg was going to be pulled off. If I had not become jammed I would certainly have been killed, as I would have been flung round and round, hitting the deck each time. As it happened, I did not break one bone; having landed right up in my groin and my leg bending the right way round the drum saved me from that. However the ligaments in my groin were stretched and I was black from my right knee to my right hip; I was unable to put my foot to the ground for two weeks.

Once I could, I was up and around again. I made sure that I never put my foot in a bight of rope again. I would never have such a lucky escape again. It was a chance in a million and I got away with it. My lucky star was still following me.

A month before my four years' apprenticeship was up, the company went bankrupt and was placed in the hand of a receiver.[12] We were directed to go to the Tyne and we moored up at a little place called Bill Quay, on the south bank, about halfway between South Shields and Newcastle. It must have been early June, because when we went ashore that evening, I called at the little pub on the quay, had a beer and asked the landlord what was likely to win the

Apprentice's Indenture
– signed off.

Derby the next day. He told me Manna was a cert. So I asked him if he would put 10s *(50p)* to win for me, which he agreed to, and I went up to Newcastle for the evening with one of the other apprentices. Manna actually won at nine to one, so that evening I called in the pub to collect my winnings to find the landlord not in a very good mood. He had put my money on for me but, though he told me it was a cert, he went and backed a French horse himself. I felt quite rich having won £4 10s, so I took one of the other boys down to South Shields. We found a nice couple of girls and took then for a walk over the cliffs. Time flew by and, when I realised the time, we made a dash back to South Shields, saw my girl home and dashed for the last train, to find that we had missed it. My pal had obviously managed to catch it. As I had a little money, I asked the first policeman I came across where there was a reasonably priced place I could find a bed for the night as I had missed the last train back to my ship. He looked at me and said 'You don't want to spend the night here. You are a young man and, as it is not far, you should walk it'. So I took his advice, he told me the direction and off I set. It was the longest walk I have ever done. It was almost all through the country and I did not meet a soul once I cleared South Shields. I frequently became lost and had to climb up the signposts and strike a match to find my directions. Three hours later I staggered up the gangway very footsore and weary and fell into bed. The things I said about that policeman would hardly bear repeating. Though we were doing nothing much, I was kept in the ship until the last day of my apprenticeship. I even had to pay my own train fare back to Cardiff to the office of the company. My apprenticeship days were over. I went home for a holiday before attending *(nautical)* school to sit for my first exam. *In fact, after one month of holiday, he started his six months initiation training as a midshipman in the Royal Naval Reserve. He did not go to the Nautical School in Cardiff until February 1926.*

After the first initial shocks I had grown to enjoy the life at sea and found it most interesting visiting many different countries. Tramping certainly was a hard life but I am not sorry I started that way. It certainly taught me to be a seaman, which has held me in good stead all my sea-going life, though what assistance I received, as an apprentice, from the officers in the study on navigation was negligible. However, some things you cannot learn from a book; practical experience is a great teacher.

It gave a great thrill when I became captain of the *Mauretania* and *Queen Mary* to receive congratulatory letters and telegrams from some of the boys who served their apprenticeship together with me, also from the mate who taught me such a lot and trained me to be a real seaman.

CHAPTER 3

THE DIFFICULT YEARS
BEFORE THE WAR

Unfortunately, there appears to be no manuscript describing these years of John Treasure Jones's life. The text for this chapter has been drawn from the following sources:
A letter, dated 13 December 1958, whilst in command of RMS Media, in reply to a request for personal background information from the Marine Superintendent, The Cunard Steamship Co Ltd;
Royal Navy Service and Awards Records;
Royal Naval Reserve Officer's Training Certificate Book;
Seaman's Record Book and Certificates of Discharge;
National Archives Material;
Biographical Data prepared c.1970;
Some handwritten notes, probably made for a speech.

I had joined The Royal Naval Reserve as a probationary midshipman on 11 September 1923. On completion of my apprenticeship in 1925, I carried out six months' RNR training as a midshipman in HMS *Hood* (29 July–28 Nov.), HMS *Velox* (29 Nov.–7 Jan.) and HMS *Ajax* (8 Jan. –26 Jan. 1926).[1]

Behind this professional, matter of fact, statement, there must have been an awe-inspiring metamorphosis: in June he was the Bosun on a 4,274-tons tramp steamer, which regularly required cleaning of coal and grain dust. In August he was a midshipman on a 41,200-ton battle-cruiser, with its acres of holystoned decks, gleaming brass and immaculately enamelled paintwork. And whilst the level of basic professional seamanship on the two ships was certainly comparable, the dress codes aboard each would have been poles apart. His Naval training over the coming years gave a polish to the hard, tough merchant experience in which his character had been formed, and this, no doubt, was to stand him in good stead later on.

On completion of the above training I attended Nautical School in Cardiff and obtained my Second Mate's Certificate in February 1926. *No doubt on the strength of this, his rank of midshipman RNR was confirmed on 18 March 1926, and on 18 August 1926, his twenty-first birthday, he was promoted to acting sub lieutenant RNR.* The same month I joined the tramp ship SS Ambassador of Hall Bros. of Newcastle as third mate.

After serving eleven months I left and did three months training *(4 April–3 July 1927)* in the Royal Navy at HMS *Vivid*[2] and aboard HMS *Adventure* as an acting sub lieutenant RNR. On completion of this, I again attended Nautical College at Cardiff obtaining my First Mate's Certificate in July 1927. I was then twenty-two years of age. In November 1927 I rejoined Hall Bros. as second mate on SS *Caduceus*, later rising to first mate.

I served in this ship until April 1929 when I left and returned to Nautical College at Cardiff to study for master which I passed on 3 June 1929. This was followed by a further twenty-eight days training *(2 July–30 July)* in the Royal Navy as a sub lieutenant RNR aboard HMS *Vivien*. *He notes that, during this posting, two submarines collided off Fishguard.*

On 18 August 1929 *(aged twenty-four)* I was promoted to lieutenant RNR. In August 1929 I joined The White Star Line as a junior officer. After relieving vessels in port *(including the SS Gallic)*, I sailed as fourth officer of SS *Euripides* out to Australia and then returned to the UK as third officer of SS *Delphic*.

HMS *Hood* (served on during 1925). (LP)

HMS *Ajax* (served on during 1926). (LP)

HMS *Ambassador* (served on during 1926–27). (Courtesy of National Museums Liverpool/Merseyside Maritime Museum)

Caduceus (served on during 1927–28). (DFH)

Euripedes (served
on during
1929–30). (JCM)

On board
Euripedes, 1929–30.

Delphic (served
on during 1930).
(JCM)

At the time the White Star was the biggest passenger company in the country, but 1929 saw the great depression set in and shipping fell on bad days. After returning from Australia in mid-April 1930, he was without a ship for six and a half months.

In November 1930 the Company sent me to do my twelve months Reserve training in the Royal Navy. This consisted of two months of Signal, Torpedo and Gunnery Courses and ten months afloat. I obtained firsts in the Signals (*HMS Victory*) and Torpedo Courses (*HMS Vernon*) and a Second in the Gunnery Course (*HMS Vivid*). I served six months afloat in the Aircraft Carrier HMS *Glorious* (3 January–3 July) and four months in the Destroyer HMS *Viscount* (4 July–31 October 1931), both on the Mediterranean Station.

He admits that he was nearly sick during his first flight. There was a story about a dummy torpedo attack on a Maltese boatman. Whilst serving on Glorious *he was present during a very notable incident. What follows is a brief summary collated from the Admiralty Archives.[3]*

HMS Glorious *had been first commissioned back in 1916 as a Cruiser, 1st Class, of 18,600 tons. In 1930 she was converted into an Aircraft Carrier as the development of airpower in support of naval operations became feasible. On 31 March she was at sea, off the southern coast of Spain, near Malaga conducting exercises in the company of 1st Battleship Squadron (less* Resolution*), 1st Cruiser Squadron, 3rd Cruiser Squadron (less* Curlew*), 1st Destroyer Flotilla, 2nd Destroyer Flotilla (less* Vanessa, Viscount, Vepa *and* Winchelsea*), 4th Destroyer Flotilla, plus seven other assorted ships. Captain Charles E. Kennedy-Purvis had joined the ship that day and would formally take over command on the following day. His only previous experience of aircraft carriers was simply one day as a guest on* Courageous *during the previous November. His chief navigating officer, Lt Commander G.A. French, had similarly only joined the ship on 24 March.*

In the afternoon of 1 April they proceeded to carry out exercises with two flights of Ripon torpedo bombers. At 14:00 they first sent up a fighter aircraft (Fairy III F – known as a Flycatcher) and the pilot reported that visibility was all clear for fifty miles. The Ripons were duly launched at 14:30 to carry out the firing exercise, supported by three flights of Flycatchers. At 15:55, contrary to the expected weather conditions, a bank of fog suddenly developed some four to five miles ahead. At this stage there were twenty-seven planes still in the air; it was decided that there was only sufficient time to land five of these.

HMS *Glorious* (served on from January to June 1931).

SS *Florida* in collision with HMS *Glorious* off Malaga, 1931.

The SS Florida *was at this time sighted some six to seven miles back off the port quarter. At 16:00* Glorious *entered the fog bank and they reduced speed. The first reaction was to turn to starboard, but it was quickly realised that this would risk a collision with the 3rd Cruiser Squadron of* Curacao, Calsdon *and* Calypso, *sailing in close order, single line ahead, on the starboard beam. They therefore turned to port, executing almost a circle to bring her back on a near reciprocal course. At 16:15 it soon became obvious that the fog bank was quite substantial and they became concerned about the dwindling fuel reserves of the aircraft as well as the possible fate of the forty-four airmen above. Speed was increased to clear the fog as soon as possible in order to allow the planes to fly-on.*

At 16:25 a faint blast from a steam whistle was heard by some of the officers, but not others, including the captain; however it appeared to be a long way off. The noise of the aircraft, which could see the ship down in the fog and were circling above, made it exceedingly difficult to hear anything. By this time the planes of 461 Flight had only forty minutes flying time left and there was no sign of clear water.

At 16:28 they heard a second indicator — the engines were stopped and then put immediately astern. At 16:30 the Glorious *collided with* Florida *before the latter's bridge, on the port side in a direction from her port bow. It was reported that* Glorious *very properly remained fixed to* Florida *until the 620 or so live passengers, and some of the crew, had been evacuated. The* Florida *was then successfully towed to Malaga, stern first, and was in a stable enough condition for the passengers to be lodged back on board.*

In the official report it states that 'Flying officer P.D. Cracroft, Royal Air Force, in Flycatcher No 14 deliberately risked a crash landing in the sea near HMS Queen Elizabeth *in the hope of stopping four battleships and seven destroyers from steaming into the already damaged ships. He was successful in this and deserves great commendation.'*

This left twenty-one planes still in the air; seventeen of the aircraft subsequently landed at the large aerodrome at Malaga; the crews of the others, four Flycatchers, which needed to 'ditch' when they ran out of fuel, were successfully picked up.

Whilst the Glorious *lost only one seaman, forward on fog lookout, those on the* Florida *were not so fortunate and the final toll was that twenty-two, mainly emigrant passengers, lost their lives. After the initial Official Inquiry, Court Martial proceedings were delayed due to the proceedings during 1933 in the High*

Court and Court of Appeal, brought by the owners of Florida *and on behalf of the families of the deceased. These proceedings found that the* Florida *had not reduced speed on entering the fog bank nor proceeded with sufficient caution to avoid a collision. Nevertheless, in 1935, Captain Kennedy-Purvis previously of* Glorious *was informed by the Lords of the Admiralty that blame for the collision was attributable to him for not immediately stopping the ship on hearing the siren, but that no disciplinary action would be taken in view of the extenuating circumstances of the difficult situation of so many aircraft in the air.*

Much of the evidence in the Court of Enquiry highlighted the massive difficulties of communicating between the aircraft themselves, as well as between the Carrier and the planes; for this they had only

HMS *Glorious* and SS *Florida*, 1931.

The bow of HMS *Glorious* after collision with SS *Florida*, 1931.

Shore leave from HMS *Glorious* in Gibraltar, 1931.

HMS *Viscount* (served on from July to October 1931).

Above left: Out of uniform.

Above right: The Bride and Groom, 30 August 1933.

The Wedding Party, 30 August 1933.

Machaon (served on during 1934-35) in 1920. (DFH)

Rhexenor, 1935-36. (Courtesy of National Museums Liverpool/Merseyside Maritime Museum)

Addis signalling lamps and Very flares to rely on. The navy at large also had to come to appreciate that an Aircraft Carrier, when flying planes on or off, needed to swing out of the 'normal line of array' in order to face up directly into the wind.

On completion of my twelve months' training, The White Star Line informed me that they were unable to re-engage me due to the shipping depression, as they had already dismissed all officers who had been fewer than fifteen years with the company. I was unemployed for a year, so worked with my father on the farm during that time.

In January 2004 there was a write-up in the Western Telegraph *on Reggie Evans, who had just turned ninety. In 1928 he started work earning 13s 6d a week as a farm labourer aged fifteen, working for Shrewsbury Treasure Jones at Slade Hall Farm. He recalls that he used to be given one shilling and a half-penny to go to Willie Thomas's shop by the Bellevue Pub for a packet of Player's cigarettes at eleven pence and a* Western Mail *for a penny. The hard toil of farm work meant rising in winter in time to*

Right: Senior 3rd Officer, *Brittanic.*

Below: Brittanic, 1939. (© Kenneth Vard & Derrick Smoothy)

feed and muck out the horses before breakfast at 8 a.m., and in summer a 4 a.m. start for haymaking; working up to six days and sixty hours a week. Every other Sunday he and another farm worker shared morning duties until about 11 a.m.

In November 1932 I obtained employment as an Assistant Superintendent Stevedore with Rea's Ltd, and was assisting in loading and discharging The Leyland Line ships at the Canada and Huskisson Docks in Liverpool. The hours were 7 a.m. to 9.30 p.m. and the pay was £225 per year. On 30 August 1933 I was married to my present wife 'Belle', *née* Lees.

The Leyland Line was sold to T&J Harrison Ltd and my job petered out. In July 1934 I returned to sea with Alfred Holt Ltd, The Blue Funnel Line, as third officer in SS *Machaon* and then SS *Rhexenor*, being promoted to second officer. In November 1936 I then left Alfred Holt as I was rather old for that company and my promotion prospects were not good. This was rounded off by twenty-eight days' training *(25 November–22 December 1936)* in the Royal Navy aboard HMS *Wild Swan*.

In March 1937 I joined The Cunard White Star Line *(who had recently merged)* as a junior third officer in the *Lancastria*. Whilst this was an opportunity to get back into passenger ships, it meant starting at the bottom again, exactly the same position as 7½ years previously!

Whilst John does not record this, he once told that he was scheduled to join Cunard at the same time as Geoffrey Marr. However John was ill and needed to delay taking up his appointment by a couple of weeks. Many years later this resulted in Captain Marr, as the ranking senior officer, becoming Commodore of the Cunard Line with command of RMS Queen Elizabeth.

On 18 August 1937 *(aged 32)* I was promoted lieutenant commander RNR. By the time the war had started, in the first days of September 1939, I was senior third officer in the *Britannic*.

CHAPTER 4

THE WAR YEARS

War clouds were beginning to gather over Europe in 1937, and then in September 1939, they broke and the deluge was upon us. Being a Royal Naval Reserve officer I was seconded from the Cunard Line to the Royal Navy on 9 September in what had previously been RMS *Laurentic*. She had already been taken to Devonport Dockyard to be turned into an Armed Merchant Cruiser[1] for the Royal Navy and I was appointed navigating officer. From being a junior officer in Cunard, I was turned overnight into a fairly senior Royal Naval officer, my rank in the RNR at that time being a senior lieutenant commander.

It is interesting to note that whilst the Great Depression had dampened his promotion possibilities through the ranks of the Merchant Navy, the Royal Navy had continued training officers and men through the RNR. In the period of fourteen years, since completing his apprenticeship, he had logged up two full years, either at sea or attending training courses with the Royal Navy.

Our first duty was to patrol a line between Iceland and The Faroe Islands in order to try and prevent German shipping getting in and out of the North Sea, mainly to stop them returning to Germany with supplies. Thus, we steamed westward on this line in daylight hours and eastward at night, by this means hoping to stop them slipping through in the dark. This proved to be rather a dull and profitless operation, though it may have had the desired effect. We did intercept one German merchant vessel after we left the line to return to harbour for fuel and supplies. She managed to scuttle herself before we could put a boarding party aboard and capture her as a prize. Their captains obviously had instructions to do this and not allow their ships to be captured. This they were very successful in doing. *This was the Hamburg America's* Antiochia *on 29 November off Iceland; the ship was inexpertly scuttled but was used for target practice while sinking.* Thus we collected few prizes in this war, the result being that there was little prize money to be shared out at the end of the war. I did, in fact, finally receive around £200 as a captain.

When we left the western end of this patrol line in the evening, the line was taken over on the eastern end the following morning by another AMC, named *Rawalpindi*. That afternoon she encountered the German battle-cruiser *Deutschland*. *Actually it was two ships – the* Scharnhorst *and* Gneisenau. The Armed Merchant Cruisers were no match for ships of this class and, in a very one-sided engagement, the *Rawalpindi* was sunk with a large loss of life. A small number were picked up by the Germans and taken prisoner.

I well remember our captain suggesting we turn back to try and engage the enemy! As she would be a matter of hundreds of miles away and so much faster than us, we would have no hope of finding her, and if we did, we would only be another sitting duck for her. We were also forbidden to stop and pick up survivors, so I persuaded the captain that it would perhaps be wiser to follow our instructions and return to harbour and live to fight another day. We would, of course, never have found this ship as our speed was only sixteen knots against the enemy's thirty-two or more. I admired the captain's spirit though. Had we remained on patrol a day longer there is no doubt we should have met the fate of the *Rawalpindi*. It was either the case of the Good Lord looking after us, or the Devil looking after his own. I prefer to think it was the former.

The *Laurentic* as an Armed Merchant Cruiser. (© Imperial War Museum – HU87352)

The Rawalpindi, *launched in March 1925, had been a P&O liner of 16,619 GRT carrying 600 passengers and 380 crew. In August 1939 she was requisitioned by the Royal Navy and hurriedly converted to an AMC with eight 6in and two 3in guns – leftovers from The First World War, one of her two funnels also being removed. At dusk on 23 November she encountered the two German battleships attempting to breakout into the Atlantic. They promptly reported the sighting to Naval Intelligence and then, refusing the call to surrender, engaged the enemy with their puny guns. Only eleven of the entire ship's company survived the massacre. The sacrifice was not completely in vain as the prompt radio report served to compel the German ships to abandon their attempted breakout. They returned to the Fatherland not to make the attempt again for many months.*

Later on we moved our patrol to between Greenland and Iceland. Here in the summer months we had no darkness and in the winter hardly any daylight. The sun used to peep up over the horizon about 10.30 a.m. and disappear again about 1.30 p.m.; these were long tedious days. We did not encounter any enemy here and, to relieve the monotony, we used to send the boarding party aboard some of the trawlers, armed with some bottles of rum. They would come back with a boatload of fresh, kicking, fish straight out of the nets. It was whilst returning from one of these winter patrols that I ran into my first trouble.

It was very bad weather when we left patrol and we were unable to fix a good departure position. This bad weather continued and I was unable to get any position fix by stars or sun, as at no time were they visible during the passage to the channel between Ireland and Scotland. There was no radar in those days and most shore navigational aides were down. Even the lighthouses showed much-reduced lights, so navigation was somewhat tricky. So we were dependant chiefly on our compasses, sounding machines, our eyes and judgement. The soundings on these approaches were not much of a guide to an accurate position. The visibility was estimated to be about two miles. I was in the chart room watching the soundings when the captain came in and said 'where are we, Pilot?' 'Here,

I hope, sir' pointing to a position on the chart 'but I cannot be sure, as this is based on dead-reckoning and soundings, either of which could be out. But I fix we are here, then I expect to cross this fifteen fathoms patch in a few minutes.' He said 'perhaps we should reduce speed, Pilot?' 'How far can you see?' I asked as he had just come down from the bridge. 'Two miles' was his reply. 'In that case we are alright Sir, as there is deep water close up to the land.' The echo sounder trace was getting less and less and it came down to the fifteen fathoms I was expecting, but instead of it starting to go up again, it continued to lessen rapidly. At the same time I heard the officer on watch give the order 'full astern both engines and hard to port the helm.' 'My God' I thought, 'we are not where I expected to be but are about to hit the Island of Islay.' The captain and I immediately dashed onto the bridge to see the high rocky coastline looming above us with the breakers at the water's edge. The ship was swinging to the helm and slowed up fairly fast, but, to me, much too slowly. Would she pull up in time? It was not to be and we gently slid, bow first, onto the rocky coast and came to a stop; it was so gentle, we could hardly feel it. Though it seemed we could see two miles to seaward, the low-lying cloud was hanging over the hilly coastline almost to the water's edge and we were less than half a mile from it when the OOW had sighted it.

Unfortunately, we went aground on a falling tide and we were soon stuck hard and fast. It was raining and blowing quite hard. My chief worry was to keep the ship bows-on to the land until the tide rose, when we could try and get off. This we managed to do by using the engines. Our bows seemed to have slid up a smooth rocky incline, but there was a nasty rock, abreast of the foremast on the port side, holding us. This probably helped us in keeping the bows-on to the shore as the tide was setting to port. This perhaps was a blessing, as, should we have become broadside-on we could never have got off under our own power. Six hours later was high water. So, five and a half hours later we started to try and get her off by going full astern the engines and manoeuvring them to try and wriggle the ship off. This was, at first, without success. The engines had been going astern for some time without any effect when, suddenly, I realised that the land was moving away and we were off. A big cheer went up and we all heaved a big sigh of relief. Now to assess the damage. We found the ship's bottom was quite badly damaged up to the foremast and on the port side, so we were flooded in the forward two holds. This found its own level and we ended up with a draft of 48ft forward and 22ft aft. We proceeded slowly to Belfast where we were eventually repaired. *She was out of service for six weeks.*

A Court of Enquiry was held with the captain and me, of course, being on the wrong side of the table – we were exonerated. Until I retired from the sea I occasionally had dreadful dreams that I was running my ship ashore and used to wake up in a bath of perspiration to find that was well.

After repairs were finished we were sent to patrol in more equitable surroundings between Portugal and the Azores. Here we enjoyed good weather, but found no excitement until November 1940. Our base was still Liverpool as we were a coal burner and this was the most suitable port to coal us. It was 4 November and we were about three hundred miles west of Ireland, returning to Liverpool. We were always routed well clear of Ireland as it was neutral and full of German spies. Though the southern Irishmen fought in our services alongside us, the fact that their country was neutral, was, I am sure, a factor that made us lose many more ships and seamen than we would have, had we had the facilities of their ports and the protection of their coastline.

The time was 10 p.m. I had just finished my coffee after a late dinner, as I had been fixing the ship's position by star sights earlier. I received a message that the captain wished to see me in the chart room. When I arrived there he had signal in his hand. 'Have you seen this, Pilot? I found it lying on the chart table.' It was an SSS to the effect that a ship had been torpedoed in a certain position at about 9 p.m. I replied that I hadn't. 'How far is it from us, Pilot?' I quickly checked and replied, 'about where we are now Sir.'

I had hardly finished saying this when there was a terrific shudder and the sound of an explosion. The lights all went out. 'Hell, we have been torpedoed!' I said and dashed up to the bridge, quickly followed by the captain. 'Action Stations' were sounded immediately we were struck.

We were unable to get in communication with the engine room so assumed that we had been hit there. This proved to be correct; the chief engineer appeared very shortly to report that the engine room was flooded and that they had drawn the fires under the boilers and our engines were out of action. The ship soon started to take a list, so I suggested to the captain that we sent some men to get them over the side before we listed too far to do so. To my amazement he ordered the commander to go to 'Abandon Ship Stations'; this was not what I meant at all. We were now almost stopped in the water and a sitting duck for further torpedoes. I soon sighted the U-boat on the starboard bow, swinging round to point at us again. I alerted the Director Layer to fix on the target and inform the guns. He informed me that there was no reply from the guns – apparently everyone had gone to the 'Abandon Ship Stations'. I called for those on the bridge to follow me to the gun on the foredeck. As I stepped off the bridge ladder onto the gun deck, there was another terrific explosion underneath me and debris flew everywhere, but I was unhurt. There was no one with me when the debris cleared, so I returned to the bridge only to find no one there. The second torpedo, striking where it did, took the list out of the ship and she floated upright, on a fairly even keel. The only thing left for me was to proceed to my 'Abandon Ship Station' which was the port sea-boat. It was almost in the water when I arrived there. My 'Doggie', the nickname for the midshipman attached to me for navigating, was in charge. When he had the boat in the water I instructed him and the lowerers to climb down the life-lines into the boat. He pleaded to stay with me, but I insisted he went in the boat. He was a grand young man who I hope survived the war and is now leading a successful and happy life.

I then went round the remainder of the stations looking for the captain and the commander. All the boats had gone from the falls, except one which was hanging on, end over the side where the second torpedo had struck. The explosion had obviously unhooked one end of the boat and thrown its occupants and all its equipment into the water. There was no one left on the boat deck, but on the after deck, where there was one extra boat lashed and stowed on one of the hatches, there were about sixty men and a couple of RNR and temporary Reserve officers. But no one had seen the captain or commander. I found I was the senior officer present. I left two officers and half the men there to get that boat out and took the remainder back to the boat deck to get the rafts stowed on deck there into the water, and try to get the boat that was hanging over the side into the water. This we did, but it soon filled with water as we had to drop it end-on. However we found more oars, buckets and equipment for it and soon had it bailed out; it was leaking badly, though, by bailing, we could overcome it. We were about forty officers and men still aboard, so we put most of them in this boat with Lieutenant Commander Wilford in charge. I said that I, with a small party, would remain aboard as I did not think the ship would sink. I instructed Wilford to lay-off, but within hailing distance in case we should need him. We had some good rafts in the water on the other side we could use in an emergency.

Some time later I heard someone calling 'Pilot'. It was the captain, alongside the ship in a Carley float. I informed him that there were a few of us on board and that I considered the ship would remain afloat. We put a ladder down and he came aboard. We walked round the ship down as far as the watertight deck, which was where one could see into the engine room. The engine room was flooded, almost to the top. We failed to find anyone else around the ship, so returned on deck. Although I felt confident the ship would remain afloat, the captain ordered us all down into the boat and the Carley float. So, we left the ship and lay-off, intending to go back aboard at daylight if she was still afloat. It was now about 3 a.m.

About two hours later there was another explosion in the aft-end of the ship. The U-boat must have come back and given her another torpedo. She soon put her stern under and the bow slowly came out of the water until the whole fore part with the two funnels was sticking vertically out of the sea. Then, with a thunderous roar, she disappeared for ever, with her stem being the last part of her to go under.

Up to this moment I had not given thought to myself except at one stage when I went down to my cabin and put some photographs of my wife in my pocket – she would be with me to the end. As soon as the ship disappeared an extreme feeling of loneliness came over me. One vivid memory sticks in my mind, yet it was a little thing. When we got into the water in the Carley float I expected it to feel very cold but it felt quite warm to me; this I will never understand as the water temperature was 52°F *(11°C)*.

The horizon, when viewed from sea level, is not very far and we appeared to be alone on the ocean. Later on we came across another Carley float with one three-badge able seaman on it; we came alongside and I suggested we split up into two even lots. None from the captain's float seemed keen to get into the other, so I did, as it made more room. A few hours later I saw what I thought was a periscope coming out of the water. So, knowing that the U-boats often took the senior officer as a prisoner, I started to rip the gold braid off my sleeves as I was the only one with any gold braid on; the captain had on an old white sweater. I soon stopped doing so as the bridge of a destroyer soon appeared under what I had thought was a periscope. It was British and we were pleased to see her. My float mate refused to let me paddle an oar and he pulled our float alongside, with me sitting in the other end as if I were an admiral. We did not realise it at the time but, when we got out of the water in which we had been sitting for some time, we felt darn cold and we had a little difficulty getting our legs to perform properly, as if we had been on a really good bender *(drinking session)*. Aboard our rescue ship we tried to find out who was missing. I enquired about our senior 2nd engineer, an elderly man, and was informed that he had last been seen leaving a Carley float and swimming away saying 'I am off to America'. What a relief it was to meet him ashore; he had been picked up by one of the other destroyers.

Summoned by the Laurentic's *distress call, the Blue Funnel Liner* Patroclus *eventually appeared on the scene in the dark hours of the morning, with lights hung over her side to let the survivors know that help was at hand. She was not to know that the submarine was still in the area and she too was sunk but not until five or six torpedoes had been fired into her. The loss of lives on the AMC* Laurentic *amounted to about forty-nine officers and crew, with a further seventy-nine in* Patroclus. *The 367 survivors from the* Laurentic *were adrift for about six hours.*

They were torpedoed by the German Submarine U99. The captain, 'Silent Otto' Kretschmer, was credited with sinking more tonnage of allied shipping than any other U-boat commander. The U99 sank thirty-nine ships in her career, and Kretschmer was decorated by Adolf Hitler with 'Oak Leaves to the Knights Cross', later increased to 'Swords and Oak Leaves to the Knights Cross' – equivalent to the British Victoria Cross. In the following year the U99 was scuttled, south-east of Iceland, after being depth charged by HMS Walker; *three men lost their lives but forty survived.*

Once back ashore, after sending a telegram to my wife to let her know I was OK, my first thought was for a bath and change of clothing. I proceeded to enter the first bathroom I came across in the hotel we were billeted in. To my amazement, when I entered, there was a beautiful female vision, standing up in the nude, drying herself. She let out a little shriek; I said 'sorry Sir' and quietly retired; would you believe it!

An enquiry was held next day and before we all went on leave, and the captain asked me what I would like to do next. Without hesitation, I replied 'get me command of an anti-submarine vessel, if you can; I want to get my own back on those U-boats'.

After four weeks at home, my next appointment came through and I was elated with it. I was instructed to take command of HMS *Sunflower*, a Flower Class Corvette. At last I was to have a ship of my own. She was completing building at *(Smith's Yard)* Middlesbrough. She was only a small craft: 203ft long, 16ft draft of 1,100 tons and could do 16 knots. Fitted with one

HMS *Sunflower*. (© Imperial War
Museum – FL4520)

4in, low angle, gun to fight a U-boat on the surface and with ASDIC, or Sonar as it is now
called, for detecting U-boats under water; this had a maximum range of 3,000 yards. To attack
submerged U-boats we were fitted with depth-charge throwers which could fire a pattern of
ten depth-charges in each attack. These we could set with depth settings of up to 500ft. This
was considered as deep as it was safe for a submarine to go in those days. Later the U-boats
were diving as deep as 800ft when attacked and getting below the explosions. In response we
were later able to explode them deeper.

This command proved to be a real challenge. It was mid-winter. Ninety per cent of my crew
had not been to sea before. They had been called-up, done a little training in barracks and then
sent to man the ships. They were strengthened and knit together by a small number of trained
ratings and naval pensioners. I had three officers plus an Engine-room Artificer, who was in
charge of the engine and boiler rooms, with a stoker petty officer to assist him.

Of my three officers, only one had been to sea as an officer and he had just joined the Royal
Naval Reserve prior to the war. He was Sub Lieutenant Tom Fanshawe, aged twenty-one. He
proved to be a grand fellow, who, after the end of the war, turned over to the Royal Navy and is
at present holding the rank of commodore RN. My second officer was little older; his name was
Buster Brown. His only sea experience was that he had served six months on the lower deck in one
of the battleships, then been sent to an officer training college for 3 months; this was his first ship
as an officer. He also proved to be a great fellow who also turned over to the Royal Navy after the
war and reached the rank of commander. He was promoted to this rank the same day as I was to
captain in the Royal Naval Reserve; unfortunately he was later invalided out and died in 1963.

My third officer was a fine handsome young man of nineteen from London, named Sinclair.
He had joined-up straight from school, done six months on the lower deck as a rating,
followed by three months at an officer training college before being appointed to my ship.
He also proved a great young fellow although I never heard what happened to him after we
parted. They were three grand young men in whom I soon had the utmost confidence. I was
Daddy to these men as well as captain, since I was thirty-five at the time.

Thus, we sailed from Middlesbrough in January 1940 for Tobermory, to work-up before
being sent to join a group on ocean escort of convoys. To start with I had difficulty in finding
three men who could steer the ship, and as we had encountered bad weather as soon as we had
put to sea, most of them were seasick. Fortunately we encountered no enemy and we came
safely to Tobermory, a little port of one of the islands on the west coast of Scotland. A couple
of weeks here training my crew and we felt we were ready to face the enemy. They were a
fine lot of young men, keen to learn and to get to grips with the enemy.

Admiral Stevenson, known as 'Monkey Stevenson' because he was rather small and quite
hairy, was in charge of working-up escorts. He used to personally inspect each escort and put

Ship's complement, HMS *Sunflower*, 1941.

John and Belle aboard HMS *Sunflower*.

the captain and crew through a stiff test before letting us go. After we had been put through our paces, he asked me what I thought of 'young Fanshawe', my first lieutenant. He was, I believe, either a relative of his or their families were close friends. I thought highly of Fanshawe and told the Admiral so. With a grin on his face, he said 'a bloody fool, keep an eye on him'. He proved to be no fool – Fanshawe I mean, not the Admiral!

My first assignment was to proceed to Holyhead, pick up two submarines there, escort them on the surface to ten degrees west and say goodbye to them. One was the very large Free-French submarine *Surcouf* that carried a small plane. The other was a British submarine that had sunk on trial prior to the war with a big loss of life; she had been recovered and re-named. Both of these submarines were eventually lost during the war.

After completing this mission, we joined up with B1 Group at Londonderry and were pitched into the Battle of the Atlantic. We were one of the luckier groups, and, somehow, seemed to avoid the U-boats. Though this was somewhat unexciting, the object was to escort the convoys through safely and this we were doing. At first we only escorted convoys as far as fifteen degrees west as the U-boats all seemed to be east of that. When they learnt that we only escorted them that far, they went further west and it was not long before we were escorting them to thirty degrees west and handing them over to Canadian escorts. We then went into Reykjavik to refuel before coming out to pick up an eastbound convoy from a Canadian group. Eventually we escorted them to fifty degrees west and used Argentia, a US base, to refuel.

My first brush with the enemy came in June 1940. It happened this way. I had been instructed by Captain 'D' to take our four corvettes out and join up with an outward Gibraltar

Flower Class Corvette escorting convoy.

Convoy.

convoy, as additional escorts. These particular convoys were being heavily attacked by U-boats west of the Bay of Biscay and the Portuguese coast. As France was occupied by the Germans, they operated search aircraft and their U-boats from Lorient, with the aircraft searching and finding the convoys, then homing the U-boats on to them. This was before we were fitted with radar and the U-boats used to come in on the surface and attack during the dark hours. They dare not attack in the daytime, but at night we had little defence against them. When these corvettes were designed it was not envisaged that U-boats would attack on the surface, in the dark. ASDIC was not much good against them when they operated like this and we had great difficulty in seeing them visually, as they only had their conning tower above the water, whilst the ships were much easier to see, silhouetted against the horizon and sky. Thus, the first we knew of a U-boat's presence was a ship being torpedoed. We would then fire star-shells and try to light up area to sight them, or force them under and bring our ASDIC into play.

When we joined up with the convoy outside Londonderry, I found, to my amazement, that I was the most senior escort commander, all the commanders of the Liverpool Group being junior. They informed me that their group commander would be joining us later; he never did, so I was left 'holding the baby'. In other words, I was in charge and responsible for the safety of the convoy. This gave me a lot of responsibility as I had no experience of being attacked before, although we had, of course, exercised our groups for such occasions.

The fun started the next day, when we were west of Ireland. A German reconnaissance plane found us and reported our position. After he had circled our convoy a few times, one of our own planes appeared and downed him. We picked up the crew and I had three of them aboard. They were a cocky young lot. Germany, at that time, was driving victoriously through Russia towards Moscow. They almost laughed at us and said 'we shall soon beat Russia and England, so you will all be home for Christmas.' What's more they really believed it. They were on the crest of a wave; we had other ideas. What we did not realise at the time was how near to the truth they were, and how near to being right they were. We had a peaceful night but the next day I received signals from the Admiralty to say we had been reported and that a U-boat had sighted us. Later that afternoon, they reported that there were at least 12 U-boats in our vicinity and that we could expect to be attacked that night. We had quite a large convoy, about half of which were for Gibraltar and the Mediterranean, and the other half for the west coast of Africa and South America. We had orders to detach the African/South American section at dusk, without escort. We escorts were to remain with the Gibraltar section and, at daylight the following day, I was to take my section of the escorts and rendezvous with a homeward convoy. I disliked having to send the one half of the convoy away without any escorts, but orders were orders. This later proved to be the right policy. The U-boats obviously did not notice them slipping away and, as far as I know, they were not attacked – but we were.

My policy was to send an escort out to the horizon on each bow and quarter about two hours before dark, to keep the U-boats submerged. Then to join and take up their close screening position after dark, thereby making it, we hoped, difficult for the U-boats to find the convoy in the dark. This did not work, as about 2 hours after dark there was an explosion and the rear ship in the left-hand column was torpedoed. It was a very dark night but a clear sky. We immediately illuminated the area and a U-boat was sighted on the port quarter of the convoy by the escort there who gave chase, made it dive and then attacked it with depth charges.

In the meantime the Commodore ordered the convoy to do two emergency turns to starboard. One turn was forty-five degrees, so this altered the convoy course ninety degrees. This was done by fixed green lights; when the lights went out the ships altered course together. We were using our ASDIC to listen for hydrophone effect. Submarines on the surface used diesel engines. The convoy had completed their second emergency turn when my ASDIC operator reported diesel engines on the port side. I glued my binoculars in this direction and there, just forward of my port beam, was a U-boat steaming in the same direction, on the surface, about half a mile away.

A Cierman U-boat underway.
(© Imperial War Museum
– HU86149)

It was the wash I could see more than the sub. I immediately ordered 'full speed' on the engines and turned the ship towards the sub to try and ram it. At the same time I ordered the gun to load with semi-armour piercing shell. Also to train it right ahead and depress it until it was just clearing my bow, aiming into the water just ahead of the ship. The depth-charge crews were ordered to put shallow settings on, which would explode them at 50ft. I had some 'snowflake' left on board from trials we had just done prior to sailing; these were rocket flares which exploded in the air and parachuted down slowly. By the light of these we could see the sub about 50 yards ahead of us and we were very slowly gaining on him. Then our flare machines jammed and we were left in complete darkness. In fact, I was completely blind and could not even see my hand in front of my face. The last I saw of the U-boat it was close ahead of me starting to dive. The gun kept firing and I ordered 'stand by to fire depth-charges'. I was going to have a guess as to when to drop them. My ASDIC operator, who was trying to gain contact with the U-boat, implored me not to fire them, as it would ruin his chance to do so. I stupidly listened to him and did not give the order to fire. He failed to gain contact and the U-boat got away. We must have given him a hell of a scare, but that was no satisfaction to me. I had missed a chance to sink a U-boat and I could only blame myself. Unfortunately, although we had had a searchlight fitted for some months, we were unable to get the requisite electric bulb for it, so it was useless. We tried our 10in and Addis signalling lamps, but they were not effective enough to be of any help to us. By now we had lost touch with the convoy and the other escorts in the dark.

Shortly afterwards we picked up more hydrophone effect, and again I could just see a wash and wake in the water. I again went to full speed and turned the ship to ram. I was just a few seconds from doing so when I made out the silhouette of one of our escorts. I just managed to avoid ramming her. It was *Alisma*, one of my own group. That was a near squeak. We heard one more explosion after this and later came across wreckage and men clinging to it in the water.

One of these was the captain of the ship. He shouted to me that a U-boat had surfaced a few minutes ago ahead of me, but we failed to contact him and came back to pick up what survivors we could find. We rescued the captain and a few of his crew. He told me that his ship was loaded with coal had sank almost immediately and they had no chance to get the boats away. *Alisma* and I cruised around and tried to find the convoy, but failed to do so. When dawn broke the only ships to be seen were my other three escorts scattered around the horizon, but no sign of the convoy. I then got in touch with the senior officer of the Liverpool Escort Group, who was fortunately with the convoy, and told him I had to leave with my escorts, as ordered, and it was all his and wished him luck. We lost two ships that night and attacked three U-boats with results unknown. The convoy was attacked again the following two nights and lost quite a few ships.

I held a post-mortem with my officers and key-ratings the next morning to go over our actions and mistakes, so we would learn from them and not make them in future. That night taught us a lot. We were all bitterly disappointed we had let our first U-boat get away, and no-one more so than I.

A few weeks later we were issued with our bulb for the searchlight; we went in for a refit and had our bridge fighting arrangements drastically altered to cope better with night fighting. It was not long before I had radar fitted. In fact, I was the first corvette to be fitted with it in our group. From then on we were able to cope better with night attacks by U-boats.

Before leaving the area I organised a search with my escorts for survivors but failed to find any more. We joined our homeward convoy later that day and proceeded unmolested back to Londonderry. Thus ended my first battle with the U-boats. We were only sorry we could not continue with the convoy to Gibraltar. *In May 1941 he notes being OC Convoy and was escorting a slow convoy south of Iceland when they heard of the loss, with only two survivors, of HMS* Hood *on which he had served as a midshipman in 1925.*

We spent our time escorting convoys across the Atlantic as far as Newfoundland. The only deviation during this time was when we took a convoy of empty oil tankers from Halifax to Curacao, waited for them to load and escorted them back to New York. There were no incidents with this convoy and this was one of two times I visited the USA during the war.

Though the Battle of the Atlantic was reaching its height during this period, somehow or other we used to get through unscathed when other convoys used to be heavily attacked. I well remember having taken our convoy over without being sighted by U-boats but the one that was following behind us, escorted by a Canadian escort group, was heavily attacked and lost around 26 ships. The escort group commander must have known his Bible well as he used to quote from it in some of his signals. One signal to base was 'Praise the Lord and pass the oil fuel; I have sunk one bastard.'

They had a really rough passage. Although we had once or twice had a slight skirmish with single U-boats and had the odd ship sunk, it was only in December 1942 when our group met its first serious attack.

The tempo was increasing. It was the third day out. We received a signal from the Admiralty stating that we had probably been sighted by a U-boat and reported. So we thought we would probably be attacked that night. The time the U-boats seemed to like to attack was between two and three hours after sunset.

If there was a moon, they attacked from the dark side, that is, from the down-moon side of the convoy, so they would have our ships well lighted up by moonlight, whilst we would have difficulty seeing them down-moon. If there were heavy seas running, they usually attacked

HMS *Firedrake*. (© Imperial War Museum – FL10040)

down the trough. When the seas were big, it was very difficult to detect a trimmed down U-boat by radar as they formed such a small target and if the radar did pick it up it was almost impossible to detect it amongst all the sea returns. So, moonlit nights, with very rough seas, suited the U-boats and were to their advantage. When the seas were smooth it was almost impossible for the U-boats to get inside the close screen on the surface without us detecting them on the radar.

That night we had a strong head-wind. There was a moon on the port quarter of the convoy. My position was on the port beam. A U-boat sighting report was detected by our H/F D/F ship, supposedly on my side of the convoy. The escort commander sent me out in that direction to investigate, but nothing was sighted or detected. The events of the next few hours indicated that the U-boat must have been on the reciprocal bearing.

About two hours after dark, two ships were torpedoed on the starboard side of the convoy. We were ordered to carry out our pre-planned search for the U-boat whilst the destroyer escort in the position astern of the convoy sighted a U-boat close astern of the convoy. It submerged and destroyer attacked it with depth-charges, but then lost contact and was unable to regain it. The policy of U-boats was, after making their attack, to dive under the convoy where their chances of being detected by ASDIC was very small due to all the ASDIC echoes we got from the ships of the convoy and for a mile or so astern from their wakes. Many a submarine eluded us this way, as it was the close escorts' duty to stay with the convoy and not remain behind looking for the U-boats. The escorts stayed behind whilst they were in contact with the U-boat and tried to destroy it, but, as soon as we lost contact, our orders were to rejoin and take up our screening position. The rescue ship and one escort were detailed to pick up survivors from the torpedoed ships.

By 1 a.m. things were quiet again and we were all back in our screening positions. The rest of the night passed peacefully. During the day we had some rest as the U-boats never attacked in daylight due to the fact that they would have to do a submerged attack. This meant that they would have to position themselves ahead, or on the bows of the convoy, and wait for the convoy to approach them. Their maximum speed underwater was ten knots and that only for two hours, and then they would have to surface. At very slow speeds of two knots they could remain submerged for up to forty-eight hours, when they would have to surface to recharge their batteries before they could dive again. On the surface they could do up to eighteen knots and the Flower Class Corvette was not fast enough to catch them. Thus there was always one or two destroyers attached to each escort group. Our group had two destroyers, HMS *Firedrake* *(1,350 tons, built 1934)* and one of the forty American destroyers built for the First World War which Britain obtained from the USA in the early days of the war in exchange for naval bases in Newfoundland and the West Indies *(HMS* Ripley*)*. We referred to them as the 'four stackers'. Though we had a great deal of breakdowns with them, they filled a vital gap in our escort force in those early years. They rolled like the very devil and I have seen them roll their bilge-keels out of the water.

A Flower Class Corvette was far more comfortable and seaworthy. Our four corvettes were *Sunflower, Pink, Kingcup (or* Loosestrife*)* and *Alisma*, manned by Australians. Thus there were six ships to try and protect sixty merchant ships – quite a task.

The day passed without incident, the barometer was falling and the wind and sea were increasing. We were girding ourselves for another battle that night and we were not long left in doubt. It was dark by 5 p.m. and at around 7 p.m. two ships were torpedoed, followed shortly afterwards by another two. These were again on the starboard side of the convoy. Once more the U-boats had got inside the screen undetected, or had fired a salvo of torpedoes from outside the screen into the mass of the convoy. Firing this way, from on the bow of the convoy, most torpedoes would find a target. Thus, if they missed the ships in the first column, they would hit in the second, third or fourth columns; this way rear ships in the columns sometimes were hit. This happened on this occasion. Two ships of the outside column and two of inside columns towards the rear of the convoy were hit. Unfortunately we were unable to detect the

Corvettes of B9 Group, moored at Londonderry between convoys. *Sunflower* (third from left) with *Alisma*, *Dianella*, *Kingcup*. Note the loaded depth-charges launchers and the covered light machine guns on the stern deck of the ship in the foreground. The white areas are where the official censor has painted out security sensitive material, like the identification numbers of the ships and installations on the coast behind.

attackers. Two of the corvettes were detailed to look after the torpedoed ships, two of which were still floating. Later they sank and the survivors were picked up.

As two escorts were away, the senior officer reorganised the screen. Two escorts were stationed ahead, on the bows, I was stationed to protect the port quarter and the rear of the convoy, whilst the SO in *Firedrake* took up position on the starboard beam as this was the most likely direction on any further attack, as it was down-moon from the convoy.

Around 11 p.m. I sighted a flare or star-shell on the starboard side of the convoy. I immediately tried to report it by Radio Telephone to the SO in *Firedrake*, but could raise no reply from him. It dawned on me that he had been torpedoed. As I was next in command of the escort group, I told *Alisma*, who was next senior to me, that I feared *Firedrake* had been torpedoed and that I was proceeding out in that direction to investigate. By now it was blowing a gale *(in fact, a force-12 storm)* and the seas were becoming quite high, making things difficult to detect any object by radar. After searching for a short while I could find no trace of *Firedrake*. There were now only two escorts with the convoy and two slowly rejoining from astern after picking up survivors. I decided I must return to try and protect the convoy and must leave my group mates from *Firedrake* to their fate. This was a difficult decision to make, but I really had no option as protection of the convoy was our first duty. I was returning to the convoy when another star-shell was observed astern of me. Again I turned round to investigate in that direction and after searching for a while, picked up a small radar contact. I proceeded at full speed to attack it only to find, as I came closer, that it was not a U-boat on the surface, but the floating after-end of the *Firedrake*. I closed with it to find that there were about thirty crew on board. It was now blowing really hard and the seas were *(60ft)* high. I told them that I would try and come alongside and get them off and asked if they would put what fendering they could over the side to help protect my ship as much as possible. This they started to do. I asked them if they thought they could keep afloat until daylight. They replied 'yes.'

As there was a big possibility of badly damaging my ship and putting her out of action by trying to go alongside in these seas in the dark, I decided to wait until daylight and would stay in close company with them. Not long afterwards however they reported from the wreck that the forward bulkhead was collapsing and they were taking in water and sinking. In a very short time there was a rumbling and what was left of the *Firedrake* disappeared beneath the seas. We now did our best to pick up the crew that had been aboard. This was no easy task in these seas. We put scrambling nets over the side for them to climb up. They were mostly on buoyancy nets with their inflated lifejackets keeping them afloat. It was useless to steam head-up-wind to them as I was pitching so much. I did try this to start with, but without success. In fact, I think my bow came down on some of them. What I did do was to go across wind and sea, get to windward of them and let my ship drift down on top of them. This worked, but one second they were down under my bilge-keel, and the next being almost washed aboard over the bulwarks. It was at that moment that my crew would grab them and haul them aboard. Some of my crew went down the nets to help those up the ship's side who were unable to climb up due to exhaustion or injury. By these means we got on board two who were unconscious; they were lying in the buoyancy nets with their lifebelts on. One proved to be dead but the other we revived. During all this we had to keep a good look out visually and by radar for a lurking U-boat.

We nearly lost the group engineering officer; he failed to grab the net and was drifting away in the darkness in the big seas. I had a searchlight trained on him in spite of the risk we ran of showing ourselves up to the U-boat. We very nearly lost sight of him a couple of times. If we had done so our chances of finding him again in those seas in the dark were very remote. I eventually got the ship alongside him and we picked him up. He was lucky.

I found out from the survivors that *Firedrake* had been struck just abaft the bridge in the boiler room and that she had immediately broken in two. The fore part capsized, trapping everyone who was in that part of the ship, which was almost all of the crew. It was only those who lived aft or were on duty there who survived.

Initially thirty-five survived the torpedoing but only twenty-seven managed to get on board, but one died later. There were 168 of the Firedrake's *crew lost and three others who had been picked up earlier who had survived an earlier sinking that night. The sinking of the* Firedrake *was credited to Lt-Cdr Hause in U211*

The Naval Secretary for Honours and Awards confirms that, in respect of this action, the Commander-in-Chief Western Approaches initiated the recommendation for the award of 'Mentioned in Despatches'. This was announced in the Birthday Honours List, published in the London Gazette *on 2 June 1943 (Number 36033, page 2445). This record was subsequently included in Admiralty files, reference H&A 269/43 and H&A 400/43. These files were not selected for permanent preservation and have been destroyed.*

I remained there until daylight and searched down-wind for two hours in the hope that I might find some more survivors, even the forepart of the ship floating. But I found nothing and set course to rejoin the convoy as it was essential that I rejoined again before dark.

This meant going as fast as I could into a head gale and very heavy head seas. The result of this was that my bow and fore-foot was often coming out of the water and coming down on the sea with great force. We did this once too often and my ASDIC dome, which projected from the bottom of the ship, was broken off, flooding the ASDIC compartment, together with the equipment. So, from then on, my ASDIC was useless. Fortunately this was a watertight compartment. I was forced to slow down and did not rejoin the convoy until the following day.

Thus *Alisma* had been 'left holding the baby' for about thirty-six hours, with only four escorts, and one of those had its radar out of action. Fortunately the U-boats must have lost us in the gale and there were no attacks that night. After rejoining the convoy that day more trouble appeared, but of a different kind. Although we had a tanker with us, from which escorts could refuel, the weather was such that it was impossible to do so. My 'four stacker' destroyer piped up and said he was low in oil fuel. Furthermore, unless he proceeded to port soon, he would not have enough fuel to get there. One of the corvettes also stated that, because of the bad weather, he had sprung some leaks and had water in his oil fuel, and would not have enough fuel to get across. So I dispatched him to the Azores to fuel, and the destroyer to leave for St Johns, Newfoundland. He actually ran out of fuel as he was berthing his ship in St Johns. That was a close shave.

We were now left with three corvettes, only one of whom was one hundred per cent fighting fit. I reported the situation to the Admirals ashore, both at Liverpool and Newfoundland, and asked them to send some additional escorts if it was possible. They were unable to help until 24 December, when three additional escorts joined me from Newfoundland. Fortunately the U-boats never found us again. This, I have no doubt, was due to the very severe weather. This time we were thankful for it.

By this time we were all rather weary and our food supplies were getting low. We had run out of fresh provisions. On 24 December the weather started to improve and Christmas Day dawned with a cloudless sky. The sun came up in all its glory and the seas were almost smooth. What a relief. It was almost impossible to rest in bad weather in those very small ships. I remember my first lieutenant once being thrown out of his cabin, the door being open, and coming to rest with his head between the steps of the ladder up from the wardroom. Fortunately he was a fairly hard-headed young man and was none the worse for it. About 8 a.m. that day, the Commodore of the convoy sent us a message thanking us for all our help and wishing us Happy Christmas. He also stated that the captain of the ship he was flying his flag in, which was a Blue Funnel ship, wished to send me some Christmas fare for the officers and ratings. We thanked him and accepted with pleasure and anticipation, as we would have had a very poor Christmas dinner otherwise. Promptly we steamed close alongside his ship and fired a line across, whereupon Father Christmas really got to work. I do not remember all he sent over, but there were sides of beef, turkeys, plum puddings and hams, cases of beer, whiskey and gin. In fact I had to say stop or I think he would have sunk us with his generosity. I was then informed that the Vice Commodore's ship would like to do likewise for another of our British escorts that had come all the way.

So *Alisma* was sent along to see Father Christmas in that ship. We never relaxed our duties. In fact we had our Christmas dinners the next day, after we were relieved by our Canadian cousins the following morning at daylight, and then proceeded to Argentia where we really celebrated our Christmas.

We got fifty-four ships safely across, but lost six merchant ships and one destroyer, with 200 of our friends and group mates. This was the biggest loss I was associated with during the whole war.

In early 1943 he was awarded the Reserve Decoration (RD), the RNR 'long service' decoration for commissioned personnel.

I handed over HMS *Sunflower*, my first command, to a Canadian lieutenant commander in Londonderry in the middle of February the following year. In March 1943 I was given command of a Sloop called HMS *Wellington*. *In the mid-1950s he built a family house in Haverfordwest and named it 'Sunwell' after his first two commands – Sunflower and Wellington.* This ship is now moored on the Thames at the Embankment as the headquarters of the Honourable Company of Master Mariners.

She was a lovely ship to command. She had spent most of her pre-war life showing the flag in New Zealand and Australia. Built in 1934, of 990 tons, she was rather like a yacht with a couple of guns stuck on her. She was fitted with ASDIC and minesweeping equipment. However, she was not a good ocean escort; her draft was too shallow at only 14ft and her top speed only 15 knots which quickly reduced in any sort of sea. I was only in command of her for a couple of months *(4 March to 18 June)*. The only interesting assignment I had

HMS *Wellington* (served on from March to June 1943).

was escorting a follow-up troop convoy to Algiers, after the invasion there. We escorted our convoy through safely, even though we were sighted by enemy aircraft. One of our escorts sank a U-boat but we were not attacked, except by one lone Focke Wolfe aircraft. He had been shadowing us for some time, away on the horizon. Whenever he made any attempt to come closer, we let off a few rounds and he kept his distance. When he was ready to head home he increased height up to about 10,000ft and flew across the convoy. We all opened up with all the guns we had, but most of our anti-aircraft armament was close range stuff, so he was fairly safe at that height. He let go of a stick of bombs but had no hits and then headed home. This seemed quite pleasant compared to escorting convoys across the Atlantic. The troop convoys had much larger escort groups. They mostly had a support group as well as close support, which made them much more difficult for U-boats to shadow the convoy or get in close enough to attack. As escorts became more plentiful, support groups were sent with Atlantic convoys until they were through the worst areas.

In June 1943 the *Wellington* and her group were ordered to go to Freetown, West Africa, and a senior commander RN was appointed in command of the group and given command of *Wellington*. I was sent on leave from Londonderry to await my next appointment. I lived in the little town of Haverfordwest in Pembrokeshire. It took me thirty hours to do the journey home. When my wife met me at the station, she informed me that Captain 'D' Londonderry had been on the phone to say that I was to return forthwith to Londonderry. It was a bit of a blow after that long tedious journey and I had been looking forward to a few days at home. Anyhow, there was no train until the next morning, so I had one night at home. My sea-trunk had not travelled with me on the train and when I arrived home it had still not arrived. It turned up on the next day's train, just before my train was due out, so I caught it by the skin of my teeth.

When I arrived at Londonderry thirty hours later and saw Captain 'D', I was informed that I was to go down and take over command of a captain class frigate, named *Baynton*, a destroyer escort built in Boston, USA. The ship was to sail almost immediately, but was to do some exercises before joining up with a convoy. Captain 'D' also told me that as time was so short, the present captain could remain in command until I knew the ship and was happy about taking over. Whilst exercising that morning I took everything in, and, by the time we came into harbour to top up with fuel, I felt quite happy to take her over. The present captain had been overseas for some time and, I felt sure, would like some leave. I also had a premonition that I might get a chance at a U-boat again this voyage. I signalled Captain 'D', asking permission to take over before we sailed and land the captain I was to relieve. We were on station, about to leave when the answer came, agreeing. So I immediately took over and gave the other captain ten minutes to pack his gear, which he did; I landed him in the oiler and took the ship out to join up with the convoy.

The *Baynton* was the first of its class to join the Western Approaches Escort Forces under 'lease-lend' in 1942. She was speedy, able to do 21 knots, and well-armed and equipped. It was all American equipment. The radar was excellent and the bridge well laid out. For the first time I had depth-charges which could be set down to 500ft. The deepest depth settings I had had before was 250ft. U-boats, when attacked, were now diving down to 700ft.

The escort group I joined up with were a Liverpool group that I had not worked with before. But the screening, searching and action to be taken when attacking were all laid down in the Western Approaches Orders and they were only varied a little by the various group commanders.

I was ordered to take up the screening station on the starboard beam on the convoy. I was allocated as an additional escort to this group for the outward passage, with instructions to proceed to Boston on completion to have new bearings fitted to my diesel engines as they were badly worn. The ship was powered by diesel electric motors, so I was a bit of an 'odd body' to this group commander. We did not know each other personally either, though I knew one or two of his commanding officers. This was a good crossing as far as the weather went. We had quite a lot of mist, which suited us fine. U-boats found it impossible to shadow in poor visibility, as they would have to come so close that they would be detected on the radar.

One afternoon, about thirty-five degrees west, I came on the bridge to see how things were going. Because of the mist, I could not see the convoy which was about 1½ miles away, but I spotted, on the edge of the fog between me and the convoy, what looked like a U-boat. I asked the officer-on-watch for binoculars, at the same time saying 'that looks like a U-boat there.'

HMS *Baynton* (served on from July to August 1943).

Commander RNR, 1943.

Before I could get the glasses on it, it disappeared; almost at once the radar operator reported that he had a target on this bearing, but it disappeared. To me it was a U-boat. The ASDIC operator was ordered to sweep an arc in that direction and he reported an echo and classified it as a submarine. I reported this to the senior officer and went into attack quickly, as it was in a position to attack the convoy and could possibly have seen it. I completed two, what I considered, fairly accurate attacks with depth-charges; the first with a shallow pattern, the second with a medium setting. To my amazement, none of the other escorts had joined in the hunt with me. The target was deeper on the second attack, so for the third I ordered the deepest setting. The target was moving on a steady course at about 2 knots. We lost contact at 500 yards, which indicated that the target was deep. I had just completed my third attack when the senior officer joined me. I had not regained contact after the third attack and was about to turn back and head for the position of the last attack. After reporting the last bearing and distance of the target from me to the senior officer and the course and speed of the target, he instructed me to take up a position on his starboard side at 3,000 yards and do a square search with him. This, I considered, ruined my chance of regaining contact, as he did not sweep back over the last known position. After doing half a square with me, he left and told me I could stay one hour. If I had regained contact by then, I was to rejoin the convoy.

I did not regain contact. The visibility was now down to less than half a mile, which gave me little chance of finding any wreckage, if I had succeeded in sinking the U-boat. I must say that I was a little mad with my senior officer. I was firmly convinced that my target was a U-boat, as I had seen it myself for a brief moment on the surface. But I had a feeling that my senior officer thought, as I was a new boy to him, it was a non-sub target.

The next day I received a signal from the Commander-in-Chief of Western Approaches congratulating me on being promoted to commander, my name having just come out in the half-yearly promotions *(30 June 1943)*.

The following day we were relieved by the Canadian escort group. I handed my report of the attack to my senior officer, claiming a possible U-boat, and proceeded alone to Boston. I later heard that my senior officer classified it as a whale and reported so to HQ. That, I am certain, was no whale, as I had seen whales plenty of times and what I saw visually was not a whale. It is a well known fact that whales did give the same characteristics on ASDIC or sonar as a submarine would do, except that sometimes that gave themselves away by doing smaller turns than any sub could do. There was no trace of such happening on my sonar recorder. I never did meet up with that senior officer again to discuss it with him. I would very much have liked to! Thus ended my second personal encounter with a U-boat – the verdict was a draw. But I still feel that, that day, I either sank or severely damaged a U-boat.

Next day we were crossing the Newfoundland Banks. It was a beautiful day and the seas were glassy smooth, except for the ripples caused by shoals of fish. Being alone, with time on my hands, I thought that some fresh fish would be welcome to the ship's company. So hands were called to 'Action Stations'. I told them we would carry out some anti-submarine practice using our depth-charges, hedgehog and guns. The next shoal of fish I spotted we headed for and attacked as if it had been a submarine, dropping a shallow pattern of depth-charges and firing a pattern of hedgehog. We then stopped, manned and sent away the motor sea-boat, picking up the fish that were now popping up to the surface. We steamed a mile or so away, dropped a target and carried out some good gunnery practice, returning in half an hour to pick up our boat and crew. The boat was filled with beautiful haddock and we enjoyed fresh fish for some days to come. This was not the sporting or economical way to catch fish, however I needed to exercise the crew, they needed the fresh fish and anyhow, there was a war on and depth charges were quite plentiful by then.

On arrival at Boston, the ship was dry docked in a huge dock, all to itself. It looked very lonely down there, in fact, you could not see it until you stood on the edge. It was July, and a hot one at that. It was like being in an oven, sitting on the bottom of that dock. We went into tropical rig which meant wearing shorts. I had to report each morning at the office of the naval officer in charge of the dockyard. It was like running the gauntlet, walking through the yard with all the female labour coming in: they all used to wolf-whistle at me. At first it embarrassed me, but I came to enjoy it. I stopped and spoke to some of the girls and asked them if they had never seen a man in shorts before; I had some amusing replies.

After four weeks having our bearing put right, we returned to Britain without incident as an additional escort with another convoy. *Baynton* a was fine fighting ship, but it was like living in a steel prison. There was no daylight inside the ship and a constant roar of fans. I think I would have gone nuts if I had to live very long in those conditions.

On arrival home at the end of August 1943, I was given another appointment – HMS *Dart*, a River Class Frigate, which had been commissioned in 1942; at 1,375 tons she was a little larger than *Baynton*, but not quite so fast. I joined HMS *Dart* at Milford Haven and was sent to the Mediterranean Station escorting a mixed convoy of small RN ships. On arrival, I formed and took command of the 49th Escort Group. I now had six ships under my command, whilst still commanding my own. This pleased me. Somehow I liked responsibility and thrived on it. My duties there were to escort convoys through the Mediterranean from Gibraltar to Port Said and vice versa. The Germans had been chased out of Africa; the Allies had landed in Sicily and were fighting their way up Italy at this time. Previous to this it had been impossible to take convoys through the Mediterranean. Even taking supplies to Malta had involved a great loss of ships and equipment, mostly from aircraft attacks from Italy and Crete. U-boats never proved to be any real menace here. Few German submarines entered the Med; it was mostly Italian submarines that operated here and they were rather ineffectual.

We remained here for over a year, escorting convoys, using Gibraltar and Alexandria as our bases, the latter being our main base. During this time we met up with the occasional submarine. In the year we only had three ships hit by torpedoes and these managed to reach port. Our most dangerous spot was off the African coast, between Oran and Algiers. Here

HMS *Dart* (served on during 1943-45).

we were often attacked by German aircraft based in the South of France. They used to time their attacks in the evening, around dusk, coming in low over the horizon to avoid being detected by ship and shore radar. Sometimes we would have some warning, other times they suddenly appeared over the horizon. Our policy was to have all ships at full 'Action Stations' from sunset to dark. As soon as enemy aircraft were reported, we would set up a smokescreen around the convoy, thus hiding the convoy from the aircraft so they could not pick a target. These aircraft usually attacked with torpedoes, but they had little success and lost many aircraft. By the middle of 1944 they gave this up altogether. Another spot where we sometimes met a few enemy aircraft was between Malta and Tobruk, on the African coast. These aircraft came from Crete, but they were mostly in ones or twos, and were reconnaissance planes rather than attackers. However, occasionally they flew over and let go a stick of bombs from a height clear of our anti-aircraft guns.

This was a comparatively peaceful mission compared to the Battle of the Atlantic, which was at its height in 1943 and 1944. It was almost like running a slow train. We would pick up our eastbound convoy just west of the Straits of Gibraltar, drop some off at Gibraltar and pick some up from there. Then, on passing Oran we would drop off ships for there and others would join us. And so on it went at Algiers and the small ports on the north coast of Algeria, where supplies were unloaded for the armies. Then onto Tunis, Malta, Tobruk, Alexandria and finally Port Said; followed of course by the same journey westbound.

The eastbound convoys were made up of loaded ships and most of the westbound ones were empty. Towards the end of 1944, things were so peaceful that convoys were discontinued and our escort force was disbanded. My ship was re-fitted at Malta and we returned to Britain for the final phase of the U-boat War.

HMS *Dart* in the Mediterranean (served on during 1943-45).

The Naval Secretary for Honours and Awards confirms that in 1945 he was awarded a second Mention in Despatches for services whilst serving with the 49th Escort Group. His name appears amongst those announced in the Birthday Honours List, published in the London Gazette *on 14 June 1945 (Number 37119, page 2973). The Commander-in-Chief Mediterranean initiated the recommendation. The citation reads:*

> *Commander Jones served as senior officer 49th Escort Group for eleven months under the administration of Captain 'F'. He always showed a high degree of zeal and efficiency as senior officer, both in Convoy Escort Work and in the administrative duties connected with his Group. His ship has always set an example to the rest of his Group and was rated first of all the Frigates in the Escort Groups for all round weapon efficiency. An officer in who complete confidence can be placed. For outstanding zeal, energy and cheerful devotion to duty as senior officer, 49th Escort Group.*

This record was subsequently included in Admiralty files, reference H&A 226/45 and H&A 400/45. Of these only H&A 226 was selected for permanent preservation and this file is available for public inspection at the Public Records Office, Kew, under the reference ADM 116/5231, p134.

I was attached to a senior group escorting, or rather supporting, shipping in the Irish Sea as U-boats had developed the 'Schnorkel' and were attacking shipping in coastal waters around the Irish Sea. By means of the 'Schnorkel', the U-boats could proceed, submerged on their diesel engines, with just the top of the schnorkel above water, sucking in the necessary air. They could also charge their batteries without surfacing.

This was an interesting assignment and we had quite a lot of fun. Many of the targets we picked up by sonar were wrecks on the bottom. The U-boats used to sit on the bottom and pretend they were wrecks and hope that we would not attack them. I have no doubt that some escaped in this way. But, if we had any doubt we would attack with hedgehog or depth-charges. I felt sure I had detected a U-boat sitting on the bottom in the Firth of Clyde and attacked it a couple of times. Then we ran over it slowly many times from different directions, taking continuous soundings on the special echo-sounding machine we were fitted with. This way we could get a picture of the sort of wreck it was. Although this wreck looked like, and was about the size of a U-boat, I eventually discovered that it was a ship in two parts.

We were escorting a convoy between Ireland and the Pembrokeshire coast of Wales on the night that hostilities were to cease at midnight. That evening we attacked every target we found, wreck or no wreck, and, in fact, we think we actually sank one that evening with our group. The next two days I was detailed to remain in the area and escort any surrendering U-boats to harbour. Two did surface and surrender to us.

Hostilities had ceased; the battle was over, at least as far as Germany was concerned. There still remained the Japanese to subdue in the Far East. Though this was mostly a task for the USA, Britain still had its military commitments in Burma, Malaya and Java.

At the end of May 1945 I was ordered to return to harbour to relinquish command of HMS *Dart* and report to the Admiralty in London. There I was informed that they wanted three or four qualified commanders to take over the duties of Divisional Sea Transport officers. This would carry the rank of a four ring captain *(acting-captain RNR)*. As I had spent all the war at sea as a qualified officer, the appointments director asked me if he could forward my name to the Director of Sea Transport. Although I knew nothing about sea transport duties, I said I was prepared to have a shot at it. An appointment with the Director of Sea Transport was arranged; I told him that I would be happy to accept the position if he could arrange for me to have some instruction. This he said he would do, but, that if I accepted, I could not expect to be demobilised with my age group. Furthermore, that I would be wanted for the Japanese campaign and would be assigned to the South East Asia Command. Before accepting, I phoned my company, Cunard Line; they were agreeable to me accepting this post and confirmed that I could come back to them on completion without any loss of seniority. On the strength of that, I accepted.

After a short leave, I spent two weeks at a school for sea transport officers *(in Newport, Monmouthshire)*, and was then appointed to Liverpool for a month to understudy the Divisional Sea Transport Officer there, before being sent out to southeast Asia. Whilst at Liverpool, the atomic bombs were dropped on Japan and they capitulated. This did not cancel my appointment as we were still required out there to deal with the transport of troops, supplies and the shipping of prisoners out of the Japanese camps.

Four RNR commanders had been selected for the South East Asia Command under Admiral Mountbatten who was the local Commander-in-Chief. Our immediate boss was to be Commodore De Salis who was Principal Sea Transport Officer SEAC and based, at that time, at Kandy, Ceylon. We were all taken out to some unknown staging hotel in the country and, in the early hours of the morning, whisked to a secret and darkened airfield some miles away. Here we were put aboard a York transport plane. Presumably it was a cargo plane, as the only seats in it were for the pilots and the navigators. There was a great deal of mail in the fuselage and that was our seats. We were about a dozen military passengers, half of us British and the other half Dutch. Amongst the Dutch party was one lady who was a first officer in the Dutch WRENS. She was a charming lady with a very difficult name 'Van Boetzelaer' who was a baroness. She was mother to us all, pouring out the coffee and tea, etc. I always remember her name as she suggested to me the way to remember it was to think of the boots you wear and the person who sells them to you – so 'boot-seller' it was.

We spent two weeks in Kandy, where the invasion of Malaya was planned. Although hostilities had ceased it was decided that the troops would enter Malaya as planned for the invasion. It was, I believe, fortunate that hostilities had ceased, as I heard that the Japanese knew the invasion plan, and, on top of that, a large number of the armoured vehicles were bogged down trying to land. I am afraid our troops would have had a very rough time. I was appointed Divisional Sea Transport Officer of the Netherlands East Indies, based in Java, Batavia. I flew to Singapore in a Sunderland flying-boat, from where I, and some of my officers, were given passage to Batavia in the British cruiser HMS *Suffolk*, the captain of which was brother to my boss.

Some advanced HQ units and a few battalions of British and Indian troops had arrived before us. We were given temporary quarters on landing in one of the hotels opposite the Hotel des Indes. There was no food available there but we were able to find some at the Hotel des Indes across the road. Our next step was to obtain some transport. This we did by finding out where the British Army Transport officer was. After finding him and telling him my immediate requirements he allocated me two cars taken from the Japanese. I was fortunate; I was allocated a very nice De Soto, plus a chauffeur, an Indonesian, who could speak a little English. The British major in charge of transport being taken over from the Japanese and just coming in was a great character and a fellow Welshman from Carmarthen; we became good friends during our stay in Java.

The next problem was to find living quarters, as we had to go out of the hotel to make room for the older and ill Dutch females who had been prisoners of the Japanese for four long years, some of whom were in very bad shape. Having transport made things easier and we found the army officer in charge of billeting. He was in one of the larger houses which the Japanese had used as their billeting HQ. He was there with the Japanese officer. When I told him that I required a house for myself and six officers, he gave me the keys to a house, 40 Van Heutz Boulevard, and said 'I do not know who is in it but that is yours for the time being. If you have any trouble, let me know.' My driver found the place. It was a very nice house with six rooms, with servants' quarters outside, plus a small bungalow in the same grounds. It was locked but there were no occupants. It was very well furnished. It had obviously been the home of a senior Japanese officer and, I later found out, was a Dutch doctor's house before the war *(Dr Hogerzeil)*. This was to be my home for sixteen months. Except for some Red Cross workers in the house opposite, there appeared to be no other British officers in the street, and most of the houses had the Indonesian red and white flag flying over them.

The next thing was to find somewhere, as an officer, to set up my organisation. I wanted to have this down in the docks, but there was not much to choose from there. The NOIC had taken over the only real good office block, which was the original Harbour Administrators Office on the waterfront. I had to be satisfied with a leaky roofed building close by, right on the front, overlooking the harbour entrance. It proved to be one of the coolest buildings in the docks. We then engaged some local Dutch girls as typists, commandeered typewriters and office equipment from the Japanese and we were set up. I was officially in charge of all merchant ships that came to the Dutch East Indies with troops, supplies, etc. for the forces, and worked in with army movements. This proved to be a very interesting assignment and I learnt a great deal about how the army worked. This was my first experience of working with them. We were dependent on the army for all our food and supplies.

The first month or so here was a little tricky. It was very risky to go outside the house after dark as one was likely to be shot up or murdered by the Indonesians. This particularly applied to Dutch personnel. The Japanese had done a good job on them to make it difficult for the Dutch to come back and take over. In fact they were never able to do so. We used to lock ourselves in the house once we got back there from the docks, until we left again after daylight. I personally did not carry arms, as I believed that the Indonesians were more likely to attack you if you did, in order to get arms for themselves. I was never molested. One of my officers would not go out unless he was armed to the teeth. We often came across bodies in the canal as we went down to the docks in the morning, most of who seem to have their hands tied behind them and their heads missing. It was extremely dangerous to go outside the perimeter under the army's control. This applied to all the ports we landed at in Java and Sumatra. These were two in Java: Surabaya and Batavia (now renamed Djakarta), and Padang, Palembang and Sabang in Sumatra. One of the army's main tasks to start with was to protect all Dutch civilian prisoners in the Japanese camps and get them re-housed, fed and shipped out of the country.

At Surabaya, the army and these prisoners were heavily attacked by the Indonesians on first landing, and quite a few were killed. This was the worst of the ports for this. It was believed that the Japanese had given them arms.

The only time that I felt a little scared was in the very early days when I took one of my officers with me and reconnoitred the dock area to see what craft were there that might be of use to us. We had no armed guard and I felt that, perhaps, we were taking our lives in

Indonesia (1945–47), 1938.

Indonesia, (1945–47), 1950.

Captain RNR,
RD, with service
medals, 1950.

our hands by doing this and boarding the ships. It was with a sigh of relief that we returned safely out of the area. The port was in a very run-down condition and most things had been neglected by the Japanese. It all took quite some work to get it moving reasonably well. I took it upon myself to get a barge and lighterage service going, and after doing so, handed it over to the Port Commandant.

After the initial problems and bringing the requisite forces in, the Japanese had to be shipped back to Japan; this was all done by their own ships and therefore did not concern me in any way. What we did have to find was ships to transport all the Dutch civilians, mostly women and children who had been in the Japanese camps, back to Holland. The able men were retained in Java by the Dutch to try and restore pre-war administration and businesses. The ships we used were mostly Dutch ships which were under charter to the Ministry of War Transport. This process took about six months, the old and the sick and children having first priority.

The first three months were quite hectic but thereafter it developed into routine, with weekly ship coming in with supplies and the occasional troop ship with relief troops. Life then developed into quite a normal, social one. I made many good friends there, particularly with one young Dutch family, Anton and Bep Bosch and their little son, Robby. They had been prisoners of the Japanese, but husband and wife had been separated all this time. As they were young, and in good health, they were the last to be repatriated. Living conditions were far from good for them in the early days, so, as I did not really need the small bungalow in the garden, I gave it over to them. My food supplies were much better than theirs, so I often had them in for meals; I became very fond of them. Young Robby was a joy to have running in and out of the house. He was always there to greet me when I arrived home and used to call to my Chinese male servant, who I had come across early on from a Japanese ship, 'beer for the captain.' I missed them very much when she and her young son were repatriated. The house was never the same without him there to greet me. We had many amusing times trying to understand each other's language. Sometimes he would become very annoyed with me when I could not.

We eventually handed over to the Dutch and the last of us left Java on 30 November 1946. I drove down in my De Soto alongside the ship, handed it over to the Dutch authorities and was the last of the British forces to embark. I took my excellent Chinese valet back with me to Singapore, which was his original home. We said goodbye to Java and in December I flew back from Singapore to the UK for leave.

I was demobbed on 1 March 1947, then free to take up again the threads of civilian life.

CHAPTER 5

THE POST-WAR GLORY YEARS

I rejoined the Cunard Line at the beginning of March 1947 as senior first officer of the *Samaria, shortly after transferring to the Scythia until the end of November 1947. He bemoaned the fact that he was now being paid £48 per month or £576 per year in 'Civvy Street' whereas he was receiving £5 per day or £1,825 per year as a captain RNR. His last position before the war had been on the Britannic. During the period of her post-war refit from March 1947 to May 1948, John was re-assigned to her during December 1947. This was followed by a month and a half on her sister-ship, the Georgic, which had re-entered service in 1944.*

It was April 1948 when I first set foot aboard a Queen, when I was appointed senior first officer of the *Queen Elizabeth* on the 20th of that month. This was just over a year after I had rejoined the Cunard Line from the Royal Navy. I was used to ships up to 20,000 tons, but this really took my breath away. She was huge, and really appeared so to me; the twenty-thousand tonners seemed like tug-boats compared to this. Here I was, senior officer, and I did not know my way around. I had to set to and learn all about her as quickly as possible as I would be in charge of her for eight hours a day at sea, tearing through the water at 29 knots. I was, of course, quite used to being in charge of a ship, having commanded several in the Royal Navy for the past five years. It came a bit hard though, having to step back to 4th from the captain. In fact, I felt it so much that I almost resigned and went into business ashore. But then I thought better of it and am glad I did so.

For the first few days aboard I went very carefully round the ship making sure I did not get lost. It would have looked very bad if the first officer had to ask a steward how to return to his quarters. Naturally I studied the plans thoroughly and soon knew all about her tanks, accommodation, her holds, storage spaces, etc. Once we were underway one soon became used to the feel of her and how she behaved in the various seas.

As senior officer of the 12 to 4 o'clock watch in the afternoon and the middle of the night it was very necessary that this should be so. One had to judge, in good time, when it was necessary to start reducing speed as the seas came up, to avoid the ship pitching too heavily, putting her bows under and, perhaps, doing some serious damage. We always reduced speed before the ship started to do this. With a ship of this size and travelling at such high speeds, the engineers on watch needed a little time to make such a drastic reduction in speed and one had to allow for this. I can well remember when I was a junior officer and we were in very bad head-sea, the senior officer did not reduce speed in time and along came a very large sea. The fore-part of the ship, almost up to the bridge, came out of the water and came down with a terrible bang. It knocked us off our feet. The result was that we had our ship's bottom set up, which was a very expensive repair job.

So there were at least two things we had to watch out for and avoid, namely, not to let the ship lift her forefoot out of the water and slam down on the sea, and not allow her to put her bow under and ship heavy seas, which could also do extensive damage on deck. Another point to watch out for was, for the passengers' sake, to keep the ship as comfortable as possible. The safety of the ship and the comfort of the passengers were always our first considerations. Before the Queens were fitted with stabilisers I have personally known them roll as much as

Prince Akihito of
Japan on board *QE*,
1953.

twenty-eight degrees either side. Unless things were well secured, this would make everything
slide across to the one side of the ship. The stabilisers made a terrific difference, cutting the
roll down to a maximum of ten degrees, except for something exceptional.

I remember being on watch one night when it was blowing very strong. I was outside
on the leeside of the bridge when the wind suddenly whipped my hat off and blew it well
out over the side. I kissed it goodbye. When I got up next morning, imagine my amazement
when I found it drying out in the bathroom. It had apparently been sucked back aboard by
the back-drafts which occurred on the leeside when the wind was well out on the bow. I may
say I was pleased to see it.

Amongst our celebrated passengers on one voyage was Sir Winston Churchill (he was the
Right Honourable in those days) and his family. Except for one or two very important people,
passengers were not permitted on the bridge at sea in those days. Winston was one of those.
I was in charge of the afternoon watch and had the pleasure of seeing quite a lot of him. He
used to come up about 3 o'clock every afternoon, after having had a good lunch, with his
proverbial cigar in his mouth. Sometimes he was in a chatty mood, other times he would just
seat himself in the captain's high wooden fog-chair in the wheelhouse and go off to sleep for
a while.

I was promoted to captain RNR on 31 December 1949. I was to attended the 'Senior
Officers' War Course' at The Royal Naval College Greenwich in 1951 and the 'Senior Tactical
Course' at The Royal Naval College Woolwich in 1956 (*'Exceptional' ability assessment*). This
was my final course in the Royal Navy.

A few months after joining *Queen Elizabeth* I was regularly taking up the position of the
chief officer. I remained with her until 1950, when I was formally promoted to chief officer
of *Samaria* and then *Ascania*. In March 1952 I returned to *Queen Elizabeth* as chief officer and,
in March 1953, was promoted up to staff captain.

During that period from the end of the war until the mid-fifties everyone who was anyone
travelled in the Queens. Here you could meet the highest government ministers of almost
any country, including Russia who always travelled with us. They had the best suites and
big bodyguards. Apart from the stewards, no one was permitted to go near their cabins. I
well remember the white-haired and venerable looking Vichinsky, and also Molotov. I recall
inviting one of their Colonels and his wife up to a party when I was staff captain. The Colonel
turned up with another male Russian, but no wife. Wives did not seem to be allowed to mix

Prince Akihito's
Cocktail Party on
QE, 1953.

with foreigners in those days, neither was one man alone. The Duke of Windsor was also a fairly regular traveller with us. I remember him in the officers' wardroom telling us how pleased he was that his book was running Nicholas Montserrat's 'Cruel Sea' a close second. *He also recalls meeting King George VI, Her Majesty the Queen & Princess Margaret, with the additional cryptic note 'brown shoes with a dark suit'.*

Mrs Eleanor Roosevelt was another we entertained in the wardroom. She was a charming lady. One thing that always remains with me was her laugh. The longer she laughed, the higher pitched it became. Before the liner *United States* was built and came into the Atlantic service, most of the US government passengers also travelled with us. This ceased once the *United States* entered the Atlantic service. Business executives, actors and actresses: they all travelled in the Queens in those days. The jet aircraft put a stop to that. But who knows, it may become the thing to do again, to cross the Atlantic by ship. I cannot think of a more pleasant way of doing so, and what a relaxing few days one can have if one so desires. On the other hand you can have a very sociable time and, who knows what romance you may meet. I cannot visualise anything very romantic happening in a plane, other than being hijacked, and who would wish that to happen to anyone!

In another manuscript he states: In February 1954 I was appointed staff captain of the *Queen Mary* and, except for the odd voyage as staff captain on *Caronia (which he was on for the World Cruise of 1955), Queen Elizabeth* and *Mauretania*, remained staff captain of *Queen Mary* until I was appointed to the command of *Media* in May 1957.

Whilst I was staff captain of *Queen Mary* we brought our young son Robert on board for a visit whilst we were docked in Southampton. He was about five years old and he had a whale of a time on board. The crew made a great fuss of him; he had all the ice-cream, cookies and cokes he could eat and drink. He obviously thought daddy owned all this as, on the train home with his mother, he turned to her and said 'Tell me mummy, why is it, daddy is so rich and we are so poor?' This also reminds me of what happened in church one day. The vicar, in his sermon, was regaling the people about not attending church these days, especially the younger ones. My wife and Robert were sitting in the front pews. The vicar went on 'Where are the young folks of today? Why are they not in church? I'll tell you why. They are out enjoying themselves in their cars, trying to live up to the Jones's.' In a loud voice Robert said 'Why is he picking on us, Mum?' A little snigger went round the church and the vicar was very amused.

Above: Vandalia, 1953. (SJC)

Opposite: Staff Captain, 1956.

On one of the *Queen Mary* crossings we received a signal from a Panamanian cargo vessel, asking for medical help. It appeared that the captain was ill and bleeding profusely. From the symptoms our doctor thought he might bleed to death if he could not have medical assistance fairly soon. On the strength of this, the captain turned the ship around and went back for him. We rendezvoused in the middle of the night and we sent our doctor over in one of our boats. Fortunately the seas were reasonably smooth. The doctor brought the captain back on board. This seemed to be a very fishy case. The doctor said that the captain was not bleeding when he went aboard, but the bed was covered in blood. He had no injury, but the captain wanted to leave. Before doing so, he went to his safe and filled a couple of suitcases with dollar bills. The doctor said that when he left, the mate also seemed to be helping himself. It transpired that there was nothing wrong with the captain. He was round and about the *Queen Mary*, enjoying himself until we arrived in New York. This diversion made us twelve hours late at New York and I estimated it cost the company US$15,000. As there appeared to be nothing wrong with this captain, I suggested that they endeavour to recover it from the owners of the ship. I do not suppose they did.

My first Cunard command was one of our freighters, a war-time-built Liberty ship. *This was probably the* Vandalia II *in 1953. Surprisingly, it does not appear in his 'Seaman's Record Book'. During early 1956 this appears to have been written up 'in arrears'. In that year there was a period of seventy-four days between discharge on one period at the end of June and the next engagement at the beginning of September. According to Commodore Ron Warwick, the normal career steps within Cunard were as follows: from the position of chief officer of a passenger ship, the next promotion was to master of a cargo ship; this was followed by returning to a liner as staff captain.*

Although I was pleased to have a command, it was something of a comedown after the luxury and comfort of a Queen. The salary was no higher than that I had been earning as staff captain of *Queen Mary*, in fact it was a little less. That part did not please me, although money is not everything. This was really going back to almost tramp ship life again. The food was far from good – there was no caviar and wine here with one's dinner! I seemed to be the only one that complained. The cook was not a liner chef; in fact I told both him and the chief steward that I could do better myself. It did improve a little after that. The navigation equipment was the bare minimum required by the Ministry of Transport. There was no radar and this I missed more than anything. I did one voyage to Montreal and back in the fog and ice. When I ran into fog in the ice area, I just stopped the engines and went to bed. I told the officer-on-watch to call me when it was clear enough to get underway again; I had no desire to run into an iceberg in the fog. Being in command of a freighter and a passenger liner are two completely different jobs. The only thing in common is to get from A to B safely. A freight captain has to keep his own accounts, as well as the crew's wages. With all the tax and *(social security)* stamp deductions, this is quite a job on its own these days. In the liners, the captain had the Purser's staff to do all this. It is a very lonely life in command of a freighter; social life does not exist.

In May 1957 I was appointed to the command of my first passenger ship. This was the day I had been waiting for all my life and, at last, it had arrived. How thrilled I was! The *Media* was 13,345 gross tons, carried 250 first-class passengers and around 8,000 tons of freight, with a top speed of 19 knots. After taking over, I had to report to the general manager of Cunard. I was fully prepared to be told what he expected from his captains. Instead, he asked me if I had taken over my ship and was I satisfied and happy with her. When I replied 'Yes', he said 'Well, she is all yours; look after her, keep her in deep water and bring her safely back.'

The night we were to take the ship out of dock at Liverpool into the river, it was blowing a strong westerly gale. This was a very tricky and old fashioned dock. *This was Huskisson Docks. It must have evoked difficult memories of working there under different circumstances during the recession in 1932, (see Chapter 3).* First we had to move into the outer tidal basin. From two hours to high tide the gate was opened. Then the outward ships started to leave; when they were finished the inward ships entered and the gates were closed. So ships could only enter or leave this dock from two hours to high water, until high water itself. Ships normally left stern first, with two tugs astern and two on the bows. As soon as they were clear of the entrance, they turned short, round close to the wall. This night the wind was blowing onto the wall in the river. To have tried to turn the normal way in this wind we would have ended up broadside up on the dock wall, and would have had great difficulty in getting off again.

The Cunard Superintendent asked me if I was prepared to sail in this wind. He was very anxious that I should, but that the final decision was mine. I said that I was prepared to, if the Pilot was in agreement with me. A little to my surprise, he was, as I knew it would be a tricky operation. I told him that I wanted him to back out into the middle of the river, before attempting to turn, and not to turn close on the wall as was usual. This he agreed to do. As soon as our stern tugs entered the river, they started to pitch and both our tow lines parted.

To make matters worse, the bow tugs were blown round the knuckle inside the cutting and their bow lines also parted. The only thing we could do was go full astern and manoeuvre into the river, clear of the entrance, as quickly as possible. This we were doing quite nicely, though we were polishing our rivet heads on the dock wall. Then, to our horror, we realised that the *Britannic*, which was to dock after we

Staff Captain, *Queen Mary*, 1956.

were clear, had come so close to the entrance that we could not back out into the centre of the river as planned, as the tide would have swept us down on top of her. My first thoughts were 'My God, here I am starting on my first voyage in command and we are going to have a collision with one of our own ships.' We took the stern-way off the ship as quickly as possible. At first I did not think there would be enough room for us to go broadside up the river on the tide, between the dock wall and the *Britannic*, without hitting one or the other. We kept cool and kept our ship's stem as close to the wall as possible and hoped our stern would not hit the *Britannic*. Fortunately there was just enough room and we cleared the *Britannic* by about two feet. I was very relieved and said a little prayer. I thanked the Pilot for keeping cool and doing a magnificent job; many would have panicked and we would have hit one or the other. It is quite possible that, had we collided, I might well have been relieved of my command for attempting to undock in that wind. But, 'all's well that ends well'. Most Cunard officials were surprised to find me in the river that morning. They fully expected they might have to embark our passengers in the dock. In Liverpool we generally embarked passengers at the landing stage in the river. I honestly hated Liverpool Docks and the system. It was so old-fashioned and tedious getting in and out.

I spent two happy years in command of *Media*. Perhaps the most interesting voyage I had in her was in the winter of 1958/59, when I encountered the worst weather and the largest seas of my whole sea-going career. We were due in New York at noon on the Saturday, but did not arrive until Tuesday morning, almost three days late. Some of the seas I estimated to be 70ft from trough to crest, whilst the average ones were 40ft. I had to heave the ship to for thirty-six hours and just ride them out. I only had forty passengers aboard. At first I think some of them were a little frightened, but, after a while, they became used to it, and when they realised we were not going to turn over and sink, they used to stand for hours at a time in the fore-end of the promenade deck, watching these huge seas through the thick glass windows, with the ship rising and climbing up and over them. They even fascinated me. Whilst I hove-to I was heading in the direction of Greenland. Eventually I decided to head for New York as the weather had improved a little.

I warned my crew to secure everything very firmly and the passengers to hold on, since, as I was altering course, the ship would roll heavily until I had her on the new course and could increase speed to make the stabilisers effective. As we came round and the seas were on the beam, three very large seas came along and the ship literally fell down the side of them. I was standing in the wing of the bridge; the ship went over to forty-five degrees, with the wing pointing into the trough of the sea. Even I was a little worried for a moment or two, and I do not scare easily. The passengers certainly had some stories to tell about that trip. *After safe arrival in port the passengers prepared and signed a Vote of Thanks to him and the ship's crew for their professionalism and consideration in such savage conditions.*

In August 1959 I was appointed to the command of *Saxonia*. I was placed on the Retired List of the Royal Navy Reserve in August 1960, having reached the upper age limit of fifty-five. I had two quite interesting experiences whilst commanding *Saxonia*. A ship of 22,000 tons, she was a 21-knotter, only four years old, and was employed on the Southampton–Montreal route from April to November. Since the St Lawrence Waterway was frozen over and closed to shipping during the winter, she did the Southampton–New York route during these months. This Montreal route was a very tough one for captains as we encountered a great deal of fog and also had the ice and icebergs to contend with most of the time. Then there was the 1,000 miles to navigate in the gulf and the river. In the early part of the season we had to enter the St Lawrence south of Newfoundland, as the northern route through the Belle Isle Straits was frozen over and blocked with ice. It was usually only towards the end of June before we could take the Belle Isle route.

The day I sailed from Southampton, *Carinthia*, another Cunard ship similar to *Saxonia*, sailed from Liverpool. This was towards the end of June. The weather and ice reports were good, there was ice off Belle Isle but stated to be navigable. I was considering taking the Belle Isle route, though, at the time I was heading for the south of Newfoundland. I signalled Captain Marr in *Carinthia* that I was thinking about doing so. We agreed to go the Belle Isle route and arranged to meet at daylight east of the reported ice. This we did. It was a beautiful morning, with not a cloud in the sky, smooth seas and excellent visibility. We could not have wished for

Media (served on during 1957-59), New York, 1957.

Saxonia (served on during 1959-62), New York.

better weather. When daylight came, there on the horizon as far as the eye could see was a mass of ice with icebergs dotted here and there. We approached this very cautiously at reduced speed, dodging the icebergs, to find the ice field was solid with heavy hummock ice without a break in it as far as the eye could see, right across our track.

I suggested to Captain Marr that we proceed south along the ice-edge on a southerly course until we could find clear water to head west and up for Belle Isle. As I was ahead, he said 'OK, I will follow you'. We steamed south for 30 miles before we came to the southern edge of the ice-field, dodging icebergs all the time. There were many of them and some very large ones at that. We steamed west on this southern edge, looking for the western edge of the ice field or a lane in it to get back north to the straits. There was no sign of a break and the east coast of Newfoundland was coming nearer. I told *Carinthia* that it looked as if we would have to go south, round Cape Race, after all, which meant putting on a lot of extra mileage and losing a lot of time.

We were almost having to do so, as the land was now so near, when we came across a break and a lane in the ice. I stopped the ship and sent an officer up the crow's-nest to see how far the lane went. He reported that it went as far as the horizon. So we decided to wend our way through this lane. We moved very slowly through the water and I nudged the first lump of ice out of the way. We started zigzagging our way through this lane with *Carinthia* following me half a mile astern. Fortunately the lane continued right through the ice-field into clear water. It took us two hours to steam through it though, and we did not touch anymore ice. It was a magnificent sight for the passengers that happened to be up early on each ship; those that were, and had cameras, must have taken some wonderful photographs or film of either the ship ahead or astern, coming through the ice-field. I was mighty relieved when we were safely through. Had it been poor weather or foggy, we could not have made it and would have had to go south, round Newfoundland, and put on 200 miles in addition to being twelve hours late. I may add that I went south of Newfoundland homeward-bound that voyage. By the next voyage the straits were quite safely navigable and we went that way for the rest of the season.

The other experience was actually in Montreal. We were within an hour of sailing, when our Marine Superintendent came to my cabin and told me that he had heard that Mr Banks, the head of the Canadian Seamen's Union, intended pulling out the crews of the tugs ordered for my sailing. He wanted to stop me sailing. He had been trying to intimidate my crew to strike for sometime, although they had nothing whatsoever to do with his seamen or their union. They very sensibly turned a deaf ear to him and his thugs. I was asked if I could, and would, take my ship out if the tugs did not turn up. I weighed up the situation carefully and decided I would at least have a try. I thought that I could do it, and if I found I could not, I knew I would be able to put her back in her berth alongside. I told the Superintendent how I proposed to do it and what I required his men to do on the quay with my lines. Sailing time came and, sure enough, no tugs turned up. I was informed that if this did happen, the tug company would try and find a few volunteers for the tugs in order to help me. It meant that I had to turn my ship right round in an area 1,200ft long and 700ft wide; my ship was 620ft long. This was quite a tricky operation. This I succeeded in doing by going full astern on my starboard engine and going ahead on my port engine, as necessary to move her stern off the wharf. Then astern slowly until I had her in the exact position I wanted, then turn her round on the engines, without allowing her to make head or sternway at the same time, heaving my bow along the wharf by lines on the shore. The ship behaved exactly as I wanted her to and had hoped she would. The operation was almost completed when two tugs came along. Although I did not need them by then, I allowed them to give me the odd push on the bow and stern as I thought some volunteers had manned them. I then found out that they were not volunteers at all, but the original tug crews who Mr Banks had ordered back into the tugs to save face, as he could see I was going to sail anyhow. He was standing on the knuckle as I steamed past, looking furious. I gave him the V-sign and said 'that to you, Mr Banks'. I had a great deal of satisfaction in this little gesture. I dislike intensely the little minorities who want to force their views on the majority.

As captain, I have always been fairly strict, but have always tried to be fair to everyone. This has usually resulted in a happy ship. An unhappy ship is never an efficient one. This, I should think, applies equally to any business or factory.

On 4 December 1962 I was appointed in command of *Mauretania*, one of the most popular ships in the company. She was the only passenger ship Cunard had built on the Mersey. Now I was moving up into the big ship class. She was 35,655 gross tons, capable of doing 24 knots. Without doubt, she was the finest natural sea-boat in the fleet; by this I mean that

Carinthia, 1962.

she behaved very well in really bad weather. She was not fitted with stabilisers as she hardly needed them. She had a great following on the Atlantic and was probably the most popular ship trading on it. Although I enjoyed all my commands, especially being captain of *Queen Mary*, I think *Mauretania* I enjoyed most of all. Perhaps this is because most of the three years I commanded her were spent cruising in the nice weather and this I really liked. We visited so many more ports, which I was able to enjoy. This was very different to the 'ferry service' of the North Atlantic, doing the same ports voyage after voyage. My relaxation was golf and I played wherever there was a course.

One of the most interesting and challenging voyages in *Mauretania* was a thirty-six day cruise from Southampton to the West Indies, via Las Palmas in the Canary Islands. We left Southampton on 14 January 1964. It was foggy and cold. It was grand to realise we were heading for the sun and nice weather. This was our first cruise out of England since before the war as *Mauretania* had spent the previous winters cruising out of New York. We were filled to capacity and would obviously make some money this cruise, which would be a change as we had lost a lot of money the previous year on the aborted New York–Naples run. (This we had started on 28 March 1963 and pulled out of on 3 October since our passenger numbers were so poor.) It seemed strange to have an all-British passenger list for the first time since the war.

A great number of our passengers had been cruising regularly in the *(P&O) Andes*, out of Southampton. Thus, we very soon had comments like 'in the *Andes* this, in the *Andes* that' thrown at us. The first complaint I received was that we were charging too much for drinks, and that certain passengers wished to speak to me about it. Naturally I saw them over this. It has always been that ships trading out of England to the East and South usually charged less for their drinks than the ships on the North Atlantic, so, perhaps it was natural for the passengers to feel we were charging them too much; they felt very strongly about it. On the Atlantic our American passengers thought our prices were ridiculously cheap. After all, we only charged 2s 6d or 35 cents for a 2oz drink. In England it would have cost double and in the USA about 2½ times as much. It is, of course, possible that the other ships only gave a one ounce measure. This I explained to my passengers, but they still did not seem happy. I eventually told them that I would report their complaint, but that if they wished to enjoy this cruise, they had better pay our prices as they certainly would not be changed on this one. What we did on the following cruise was to halve the price of the drinks, but also halved the measure to one ounce. This seemed to make everyone happy and we collected the same revenue. People are funny at times.

There was no doubt that, for comfort's sake, we really had more passengers aboard than we perhaps should have had for such a long cruise. The main problem was in the evenings, after dinner, when the public rooms became so crowded, particularly when everyone wanted to be in the same one or two rooms. The ship was designed as a three-class ship, thus when we cruised as one class, though we had plenty of public room space, it was divided up into too many small rooms and we did not have, say, two large rooms that would accommodate all the guests. The passengers who suffered most from this were those who had booked in the best suites and cabins, and paid higher prices, as they mostly dined on the second sitting. Thus, when they came to the public rooms, all the seats were occupied by those who ate on the first sitting, and they were usually the ones who had the lowest price cabins. It is only natural that those paying the high prices should feel a little annoyed. There was, of course, nothing we could do about it in the ship. Our job was to give the best service possible, with the facilities we had. All we could do was to spread the entertainment over as many rooms as possible and encourage the guests to spread out somewhat. Those who booked the lower-priced cabins had, I am sure, a thoroughly happy cruise and enjoyed every moment. I am afraid that some who had the higher-priced cabins were somewhat disappointed. For those who like cruising and sail in ships with two sittings in the dining rooms, I usually suggest that they choose the first sitting in the dining rooms, if they want to have the best seats in the public rooms after dinner.

Our cruise itinerary was Las Palmas, Barbados, Trinidad, Curacao, Port au Prince, Kingston Jamaica, Vera Cruz for Mexico City, Port Everglades, Nassau, Ponta Delgada in the Azores and

Mauretania at Tenerife.

Southampton. Las Palmas, Curacao and Port Everglades were the only ports we berthed alongside; the other ports were anchorages and we landed the passengers by our ship's launches, as well as with the assistance of shore launches in some of the ports. If there was much wind, this became a tricky operation, especially getting people in and out of the boats at the ship's gangway.

After Port au Prince it became apparent to me that possibly we would not have enough fresh water to last us to Port Everglades which was the next port where we would be going alongside. Neither Kingston nor Vera Cruz could supply us with fresh water at anchor. Although *Mauretania* had never been alongside at Kingston, as there was no wharf long enough to take us, I could take on fresh water if I could somehow get the ship alongside. I discussed this with the Harbour Master Pilot and my agent there and it was just possible to get about two-thirds of the ship alongside one of the wharfs where I could take on fresh water. I figured out that if I used my two anchors with a wide spread, I could hold the bow in to the berth with my port one and use the starboard one right ahead for getting away and to stop going too far astern into shallow water. I could only back in so far at the berth, as there was not sufficient water right in. This had to be done with the use of the helm, engines and anchors before securing the lines ashore to hold her stern. We succeeded in carrying out this operation successfully and I was able to tank enough water to take me on to Port Everglades. For the moment my worries were over, so I went ashore and had a round of golf.

Our next port was Vera Cruz in Mexico, which is the port for Mexico City. Here we lay in a restricted anchorage, surrounded by coral reefs, which channels through them. This could be a dangerous anchorage in a hurricane. From the anchorage it is about one and a half miles to the landing stage. All went well during the day, but that evening I received a hurricane warning and cancelled all shore leave for passengers and crew after dinner. The hurricane did not materialise so I felt a bit of a fool the next day for having stopped shore leave that evening. The day was nice and fine, but again, that evening, I was sent a warning from ashore that a hurricane might spring up. As I had stopped leave the previous evening, I did not want to do so again this evening. So instead, I warned both passengers and crew that bad weather was expected and that I advised them not to go ashore though I would not stop them if they wished to. Further, that if they went, it was at their own risk since, if bad weather did materialise, they may have to stay ashore all night. To my amazement there was quite an exodus of both passengers and crew. All went well until midnight, so I made out my orders and retired to bed, with the instructions to be called if the wind became stronger than Force 5. Because of the reefs in close proximity, I might have to consider weighing anchor and proceeding out to sea until the wind eased. The officer in charge called me at 2 a.m. The wind had increased to Force 6 and was still increasing. There was quite a sea running by the time I got dressed and came on the bridge. There was one boatload of passengers and crew trying to come alongside the gangway. The boat was tossing about quite violently on the waves passing down the ship's side. It looked much too dangerous to me to allow them to try and come aboard. So I ordered them to return in shore and to remain inside the breakwater until the weather had subsided. At the same time I instructed the officer on the landing not to send anymore boats out until he received instructions to do so. The people in that last boat had quite a frightening experience as the wind and seas had come up so quickly. Fortunately no one was hurt but many got wet. The ship was holding to her anchors alright, so I did not proceed out to sea.

On checking my crew in the morning we found that about half of them were ashore and it was still blowing very hard, with heavy seas running. There were also, of course, quite a number of passengers ashore who had ignored my advice. About noon, the wind and seas started to easy down and we started to try and bring the crew aboard, using the Pilot Boats which were more suited to that weather than our own. As the day progressed the weather improved, but it was 7 p.m. before we had all the crew on board. By then the weather had improved sufficiently to start bringing the passenger aboard. This did not in any way interfere with the passengers who went on tour to Mexico City. I did not get to set foot ashore here. Unless weather conditions were good and settled I never went ashore when the ship was at an anchorage.

The next day I had some repercussions from a party of four passengers who demanded to see me. They had apparently been in the launch which I sent back ashore, as I considered it too dangerous for them to come alongside and board. They complained that we had endangered their lives, that their clothes were spoiled, etc. I pointed out to them that they had all been advised not to go ashore that evening and that, in spite of my advice, they had done so. This is typical of some few people who will not listen to advice and then try to blame you afterwards for allowing them to take these chances. In this particular case, the weather had deteriorated very rapidly from the launch leaving the pier and reaching the ship. No one was injured, though one or two had been a little frightened. Again 'all's well that ends well'.

We also had bad weather at the end of the cruise. Out last port of call was Ponta Delgada in the Azores. When we arrived there it was blowing a gale, so I could only come close to the harbour. The agent's launch came out to us and we managed to pick up our mail by line from the launch. There was no hope of landing anyone there so I steamed around the island instead and then headed for Southampton.

In June 1964 I had a new experience. Earlier that year the Welsh Division of the British Broadcasting Corporation had phoned me up when I was on leave and asked if I would cooperate with them in making a television film about the life of a liner captain. This came right out of the blue for me. When I asked them why they had picked on me they replied that they had been watching my career for some time and, as I was a Welshman, they thought that I would suit the part for Welsh Television. Not being of too shy a disposition, I agreed to cooperate if Cunard were agreeable. The result of this was that the Welsh television team sailed with me in *Mauretania* on 23 June for the round trip to New York and back to Southampton to make this film. For this voyage I had the new experience of being an actor as well as the master of the Ship. Mr Selwyn Roderick was the producer and Mr Hywel Davies was the interviewer and commentator. Both charming men, with whom it was a real pleasure to work. It was with the deepest regret that I learnt that the latter died a few months after the film was shown on the TV in Wales. He was then working on a shortened version for the national network. I thoroughly enjoyed being a 'film star' even for just a short while. It meant a lot of

Mauretania at Milford Haven, 1964.

extra work, as I had the responsibility of running the ship at the same time. The film was very well received in Wales. From being almost unknown, I became a national figure overnight.

Around the same time as this film was shown I had another most interesting assignment which gave me one of the biggest kicks of my life. I was born, bred, schooled and lived in a little town called Haverfordwest in Pembrokeshire, Wales. This is a very old town with a long history. It is about five miles from the port of Milford Haven. This used to be a well-known fishing port, but in later years, due to its being one of the deepest natural harbours in the world, it was developed into an oil refinery port. First ESSO built a refinery there and then BP built a terminal and storage depot in order to pump the oil to their refinery near Swansea. Then, along came Texaco, who also built a refinery there. Texaco invited Queen Elizabeth, the Queen Mother, to open the refinery and she graciously accepted. This is now where I came into the picture – Texaco also chartered the *Mauretania* to take their guests for a little cruise from Southampton to Milford Haven and back. We were to berth the ship at Texaco Oil Wharf, from where the guests would be motored up to the refinery for the opening ceremony by the Queen Mother, who had come down by the Royal Train. After the opening, the Queen Mother and all the other guests would re-embark in *Mauretania* for lunch on board.

For me this was a real thrill. It would give me, once again, the great honour of meeting Her Majesty. I had been presented to King George VI and Queen Elizabeth when they boarded the *Queen Elizabeth* to view the Queen's portrait which was hung in the main lounge of the ship in June 1948. There was also the thrill of bringing my beloved *Mauretania* into my home waters of Milford Haven. This was something I had never even dreamed might happen; it was like the end of a fairy tale – local boy goes to sea in a tramp in 1921 and returns to his home waters in 1964, amongst his friends, in command of the biggest passenger ship to ever enter the harbour. This was a red letter day for me and a great day for Milford Haven. I was later told that more people came from long distances to see *Mauretania* arrive than had done for any previous occasion, including the visit of the Royal Yacht with the reigning monarchs aboard.

I am sure that I never had a more distinguished passenger list than we had for that cruise. The guests at Southampton were received by Sir Edward and Lady Beetham and myself; 278 took passage both ways and ninety-seven joined at Milford for the lunch. This was, in a way, a little risky operation to set up for lunch, as it was possible that the weather could have been so bad that it might not have been safe for me to attempt to take the ship in. That would have completely 'upset the applecart' as the saying goes. Anyhow, fortune seems to favour the brave, as the weather was good, except that the visibility was only about two miles. This spoiled it somewhat for all the visitors on the shores trying to have a really good view of us. We had a right-royal reception from the ships in port.

My great moment came when Her Majesty boarded the ship after opening the refinery. She was escorted aboard by the Cunard Chairman, Sir John Brocklebank, who presented me to her. From then on Her Majesty was escorted by me. My senior officers were lined up and I presented them to her; a fine lot of officers they were and I was proud to present them. From there I escorted her to her suite of rooms and left her with her ladies-in-waiting. Later, when Her Majesty was ready to proceed, I would escort her to the Smoke Room where a selected number of guests were presented to her. When she emerged from her suite she said to me 'what do you think I have been doing, captain?' I dare not hazard a guess, so I said 'I have no idea, ma'am'. Her Majesty said 'I have been writing to Prince Charles on *Mauretania* paper. He would love me to do so on *Mauretania* paper.' He must have been sixteen at that time and I thought what a homely touch that was. Perhaps the greatest moment was when all the guests left for the dining room, including their hosts, Sir Edward and Lady Beetham, leaving me alone with Her Majesty to escort her to the dining room, once all the others had taken their places. Her Majesty remarked about the ship and the lovely rooms as we passed through them. Then, that never-to-be-forgotten moment, when the toastmaster announced us and I escorted her down the dining room to her seat, and handed her over to her host, Sir Edward. I then took my place a few seats away.

After lunch, the reverse procedure, when I escorted her out of the dining room to the gangway and said goodbye. What an honour this had been for me. My mind flashed back to my apprenticeship days, with the coal and grain dust and the terrible conditions. Could this be the same person now escorting and dining with royalty – a fairy story come true.

Whilst in command of the Mauretania he also made one return voyage to New York in July 1965 as the Master of Queen Elizabeth.

᠊᠊᠊

The first *Mauretania* made her maiden voyage in 1907 and has passed into British maritime history as the ship that, by performance rather than by sheer size, kept up her passenger numbers throughout her life, and, as sometimes happens with ships, grew faster as she grew older.

The second *Mauretania*, which I was proud to command for three years, lived somewhat in the first *Mauretania*'s reflected glory, although she was, in her own right, a very fine ship, a little larger than the first but not quite so fast. I was also to be her last captain. It is a funny thing, but one seems to receive more publicity as a 'last captain' than one does as the 'first captain'; maybe that is because the ship has made herself such a fine reputation, whereas a new one has yet to prove herself. Due to the decline in passenger traffic by sea across the North Atlantic, and the fact that *Mauretania* was rather an expensive ship to operate, it was decided that she should end her life earlier than most passenger ships. She was to be withdrawn from service at the end of the 1965 season and put up for sale. She was sold for scrap to the English firm of T.W .Ward.

Her final voyage was a cruise to the Mediterranean, from New York on 15 September, ending at Southampton. This was a long but truly excellent cruise, visiting thirty-two ports, going up the Dardanelles as far as Istanbul, visiting all the major ports in the Mediterranean and taking in the Greek Islands and many of the smaller ports. To me, Venice was one of the highlights, as I had only been there once before. The last time had been in 1955, as staff captain in *Caronia*, known as 'The Green Goddess' as she was the only Cunard ship painted green in those days. That time we anchored outside; this time we went up the river and berthed alongside in Venice. Though *Mauretania* was a little larger than *Caronia*, she was a much better ship to handle. This was quite a tricky operation as it is a narrow, very winding river, with some very tricky bends to manoeuvre round, and, at the end, there was only just room to turn the ship in one place to come out again. Venice is a fascinating place. I spent one day playing golf at the Lido with some of my American friends, Bill Murray and his pals Anderson and Bennett; it was a very good and interesting course. It was quite a hair-raiser taking the ship out in the dark that night. I found great difficulty in seeing the bends because there were so many lights. The Pilots were good and knew their river, so we came out safely. I would not have cared to take her out myself, in the dark, without more experience of the place.

We duly arrived at Southampton at 8 a.m. on 10 October. I was mobbed by the press and television, as this was her final arrival. It was 4 p.m. before I could get away from the ship that day, when normally I was away about two hours after docking. Then came the final voyage, the 'funeral voyage' as I called it – taking *Mauretania* to Inverkeithing on the Firth of Forth in Scotland. The only passenger was my wife, my good and faithful first mate. *In fact, she was not a passenger in the true sense of the word, since she had to be signed-on as part of the crew with a wage of a penny a day.* It was not a pleasure cruise in any sense of the word. We had a skeleton crew, and there was just the bare linen and bedclothes necessary; there was no caviar and lobster, not even for the captain and his mate, with only the bare provisions being put aboard to get us there.

Mauretania made her final port departure from Southampton on 20 November 1965. Again this entailed a large number of press, radio and TV interviews, but by now I was getting quite used to these. A very large number of people came to the docks and lined the shores to say farewell to *Mauretania*. In fact, we had almost as big a send-off as we would have on *Queen Mary* in 1967. It is amazing how sentimental one can get over a ship, but then, nobody likes saying a final goodbye to an old friend, knowing they will never see them again. I still have my first old car, which my youngest boy now uses; I would hate to send that to the scrapyard. Perhaps I am too sentimental.

This voyage took us through the Straits of Dover and up the east coast of Britain. The Straits of Dover are now probably the busiest stretch of water anywhere in the world. The tides run fast there and there are numerous sandbanks all around. It is a bit of a nightmare of a place to navigate in bad weather and fog. It is most essential that the captain is on the bridge all the time going through there. The channels are not very wide and traffic is going in all directions there. There have been many collisions here in fog and many ships have been wrecked on the Goodwin Sands over the years. I do not envy the captains who trade regularly through there. Fortunately we did not get fog going through there, but it did blow a gale and we encountered quite rough seas.

This was not my wife's first trip with me. She had come with me once before from Southampton to Liverpool, again when there were no passengers aboard. In those days, the company would not permit wives to sail in the ships with their husbands aboard. I was the first captain to be granted this privilege. On both voyages we encountered quite strong gales, so much so on the first one, that I had to wait outside Liverpool for two days until the gale abated, as the authorities would not permit me to enter. This was the first time that this had happened to me and the first time my wife had sailed with me. My crew were saying 'It's alright for the Old Man, he has his wife aboard. He does not care how long he stays out here.' This was far from the truth, as I had some pressing engagements I wanted to keep ashore. It was strange that, here again, with my wife aboard, we ran into bad weather; it was making me wonder if she was a bit of a Jonah. Anyhow, the weather fined-up and we made it to our destination on time.

Before I could enter the channel, it was essential that I pumped out our tanks to get the ship's draft down to a maximum of 26ft. When the time came to start entering the channel, the chief officer and chief engineer reported to me that there was a leak somewhere in the ballast pipeline and that they had been unable to pump some of the tanks out. The result being that my draft was still 28½ft. At this draft it was impossible to enter as we would stick in the channel. This was the highest tide for a month and from now the level of the tides would start falling. I gave instructions to try and get the ballast pipe wrapped and bandaged, and to endeavour to get the remaining tanks out by midnight. I would try and enter on the next tide at 1 o'clock in the morning.

I consulted the ship's broker regarding the terms of the delivery conditions and he informed me that it was my company's obligation, and thus mine, to deliver the ship into berth in order to fulfil the Contract of Sale. In other words, the ship was Cunard's until I put her in the berth and if I stuck in the channel, I would be responsible. This put me in a bit of a spot. The Pilot assured me that the bottom was soft mud and that I would be able to push the ship through, say, six inches to a foot of it. Then, to make matters worse, the Managing Director of Ward's nearly threw a fit when I said that I proposed to attempt it in the dark. He told me 'This is the biggest ship we have ever tried to get in here and we have never taken one in the dark.'

I told him that as the tides were reducing, it was essential I did not miss another or we would be at anchor for a month, and, at any rate, there was always a first time for anything. Furthermore, that the small leading-lights marking the channel were, in fact, a damn sight better to see than the couple of thin white posts they had as day markers. He then stated that he did not think the tugs would help me in the dark, as they were afraid of running aground. I said: 'Ask them and if they are willing and I can get my draft down, we are going in, in the dark.' The tugs said they would come, so I decided to have an hour or two's sleep before the operation. I instructed my officers to call me at midnight and told them that I wanted to know the draft at the same time. It appears that Ward's representative and the broker could not believe that I was serious and asked my officers; they told him that if I said I was going, then I would go.

Midnight came and I had managed to sleep a little. My chief officer told me that they had done all they could and emptied out all the tanks possible, but that our draft was still 26½ft. This set me a poser. About half way there was a patch of only 26ft in the channel and, about a ship's length from the berth, there was only 23ft of water. This meant that I would have to push the ship through 6 inches of mud half way in and 3½ft just before reaching the berth. I consulted my local Pilot again and he assured me it was soft mud. So, I decided to go, realising at the same time that, if I stuck, I would have to shoulder all the blame.

Instead of making any tugs fast, I instructed two to go in ahead of me and two to remain astern of me to follow me in. This way I would have two tugs each end of me if we did stick. I did not want them to make fast, as I knew the ship would steer better without them and that I could control her better with engines and rudder. We lined her up in the channel nicely and then the forward tugs belched forth smoke and, for a while, I lost sight of my leading lights. This really worried me, but we somehow kept to the channel until we sighted them again. Then came the first shallow patch. The ship started to sheer but by quickly steering with helm and engines I was able to correct it. The first obstacle was over. There was dead silence on the bridge except for my orders. I was naturally going in very slowly. Then we came to the final obstacle. As the ship ran into the mud-bank she quickly started to slow up. I ordered 'Full Ahead on both engines' and she started to gain headway again. The wall at the head of the small dock loomed up close ahead and as the ship cleared the mud bank she quickly started to go ahead. I gave the order 'Full Astern' on two engines and pulled the ship up with about 200ft to spare and about 20ft off the berth. We were there. All I had to do now was have the tugs push her alongside the berth, and make her fast. The chief engineer phoned up and said I could not use the engines again as his condensers were full up with mud. This did not worry me one bit as I would not need them again and they certainly would not turn again in the ship. I had completed my part of the contract. I had delivered her into the berth.

Did I heave a sigh of relief! I had a good stiff whiskey when it was all over and went to bed. I had no sooner gone to sleep when the chief engineer wakened me to tell me we were leaking badly in the Generator Room, through a fractured pipe of the ship's side. I told him not to worry, but to close the watertight doors to the Generator Room as the ship would soon be high and dry on the mud anyhow and we did not need the generator anymore. When I got up in the morning she was high and dry; there was about two feet of water in the dock. When I looked at the gap we had come through in the dark I could hardly credit it was possible. Once again, luck was with me. It was a miserable wet morning as my wife and I left the ship in this junk yard. And junk yard it really was: we had to walk around it and through the mud. I hated like hell leaving such a fine ship in such a place.

This was the first ship I took to the scrapyard and I never wanted to take another ship to such a place.

CHAPTER 6

THE RMS QUEEN MARY

Whilst I commanded the *Queen Mary* from 30 December 1965 *(actually from 8 September 1965)*, it was only on 2 February 1966 that I officially became captain of the *Queen Mary* and my name was put on her register. It had taken forty-four years and eight months at sea to climb here and some American friends of mine used to say that once there, you were on the way out. How true! I had 2½ years to go to reaching retirement age. Still I was happy to have that long command of a Queen and this was probably longer than the average. It so happened that I was not to have that long, as, in the middle of 1967, the company decided to retire *Queen Mary* a year earlier than they intended as she was losing too much money. But I was very pleased to know I was to be her last captain. I actually was in command for one year and ten months, and what an interesting time that proved to be. I took her on voyages she had never done before. Firstly, a twenty-seven-day cruise from New York around the Mediterranean, then back to New York. This was the first time *Queen Mary* had ever been in the Mediterranean. Although it was not the best time of the year to cruise there, we were lucky and had good weather in each port we visited, and in most cases it had been bad the few days prior to our arrival. Because of our size, we were limited to the number of ports we could visit and in no port could we go alongside. So it was anchorage and boat-work everywhere.

One of the most interesting voyages on the Atlantic was the one in August 1966. On 24 May that year there was an official seamen's strike which lasted until 1 July. During this time the ship remained alongside, in her berth, at Southampton. This was, without doubt, what caused the company to retire *Queen Mary* earlier than intended. This strike did a great deal of damage in many ways and certainly lost the company a great deal of money.

When we sailed on the next voyage, we found we were unable to do the speed we normally could. In fact it was two knots less than our normal speed; also the ship was vibrating badly. The only cause we could think of for this was that the ship's bottom had become foul whilst lying so long without moving, shell having possibly grown on the bottom. On arriving back at Southampton we sent divers down; they could find nothing, but there was a little growth on the ship's sides. On returning the following voyage, during which there had been no improvement in performance, skin divers cleaned off the ship's side under water, but, due to so little water being under the ship, they were unable to reach the flat bottom underneath, which is a vast area.

Though there was a slight improvement that voyage, her performance was still bad and we were finding great difficulty in keeping to our schedule. It was therefore decided to put her in dry-dock on return and find out the real trouble. There was about one quarter of an inch of small shell on the ship's bottom but no heavy concentrations. This was all cleaned off and we set off on our next voyage and found that the vibration had disappeared and we were back to our normal speed. It is quite incredible that such a small thing could have such a major effect on such a large vessel.

I remember another occasion on *Queen Mary*, back when I was staff captain. One day we suddenly developed a terrific vibration. The captain stopped each engine in turn and it was pin-pointed to the starboard aft engines and propeller. It was so bad that if we had continued using that engine we might have shaken the mast out of her. The ship was already shuddering.

The Captain's Table, with his 'tiger' Whelan at his left shoulder, 1966.

We continued the voyage on three engines and managed to keep our schedule. Entering and leaving Cherbourg, this engine was used to manoeuvre the ship and put astern. On leaving we decided to give the engines another trial going across the English Channel. To our surprise and delight there was no vibration. Divers were sent down in Southampton and it was discovered that the metal rope guard covering the shaft between the boss of the propeller and the stern gland was missing. It was obvious that this terrific vibration was caused by this guard, which weighed perhaps 200lb being loose and setting up such violent vibration.

Coming back to the occasion of the shell on the ship's bottom: we had received quite a lot of bad publicity over our vibration and poor speed. I was called in to see the Managing Director to see if we could create some good publicity to counter this. The result being that I was told I could have a free hand on the following voyage on the amount of oil fuel we could burn, if I considered weather conditions were such that we could arrive a tide early *(twelve hours)* back at Southampton on the homeward voyage. This I was not to divulge to anyone, only the chief engineer, in case we were not successful. On leaving New York I studied the weather maps and the conditions looked favourable. So I explained the set up to the chief engineer and that he was not to divulge to anyone, not even to his officers, what we were doing, and I also kept it to myself. Only when I was certain that I could arrive a tide early would I let the ship know. This I was able to do on the third day out. The weather was kind to us and we obtained the excellent publicity we had looked for. It was only when the *Daily Express* representative told me so that I realised we had made the fastest crossing between Ambrose Channel Light Vessel and Bishop's Rock for the *Queen Mary*, since she took the Blue Riband. It took us four days, three hours exactly. *The* Queen Mary *had previously won the Blue Riband of the Atlantic from the* Normandie *in August 1936, crossing the Atlantic westbound in four days and twenty-seven minutes, an average speed of just over 30.14 knots and then eastbound in three days, twenty-three hours and fifty-seven minutes at 30.63 knots.* Even then we had not opened the ship full out. This gave us all quite a thrill and for once no one had had an inkling that anything untoward was up. We, of course, apologised to the passengers for any inconvenience we might have caused them by arriving early. It is not often that we had to apologise for being early! Once before I had done this whilst commanding *Saxonia* and that time I received a bottle from the then Manager at Southampton. His classic remark was 'we don't mind you being late, but we never want you early.' Sometimes it is hard to win!

The *Queen Mary's* last voyage on the North Atlantic, to and from New York, was very special. It was patronised mainly by travellers who had made many voyages in her and those who wanted to be able to say they had been on *Queen Mary's* last North Atlantic voyage. Perhaps the highlight of the westward voyage was on the day *Queen Elizabeth 2* was launched. Up to the time of launching, the name had been kept a strict secret, although we all had made our guesses at what it might be. The date was 20 September 1967. The time of the launch in Britain was 2.30 p.m., but onboard it was 10.30 a.m. Everyone, including the passengers, was eager to hear the name to be given her by Queen Elizabeth II. The ship was linked up by radio telephone to the announcer at the launch at Clydebank, and we were also receiving the broadcast of the launch on the radio. Shortly after the launching ceremony, the announcer at the launch spoke to me on the ship and wanted to know my reactions to the name. To be honest, I was completely taken by surprise. Of all the names suggested, none had been *QE2*. I had to think quickly to answer that one, and we were live on the air all over Britain and probably Europe and America. I had to be somewhat careful. I think my reply was to the effect that, I was a little surprised that it was another queen, but if it was a 'queen name' they wanted to give her, then they could not have chosen a better one than our present beautiful and beloved Queen Elizabeth II. At 11.00 a.m. we threw a champagne party in the Tourist Class, at 11.30 a.m. in the Cabin Class and at 12.00 noon in the First Class; at each of which I said a few words and toasted 'The New Queen, long may she reign the high seas, and be a worthy successor to the two magnificent queens whose reigns are nearing their end.' Everyone entered into the spirit of it and a good party was had by all. There was a great deal of discussion about the name, with many for it, and many against.

ABSTRACT OF THE LOG OF THE CUNARD STEAM-SHIP COMPANY LIMITED
R.M.S. "QUEEN MARY"
Captain J. Treasure Jones, R.D., R.N.R. (Rtd.)

NEW YORK — CHERBOURG — SOUTHAMPTON

Date (1966)	Distance	Latitude N	Longitude W	Weather, etc.
Weds., Aug. 24				At 1227 EDST (1627 GMT) left berth, Pier 92, N.Y.
,, ,, ,,				At 1424 EDST (1824 GMT) ACLV abeam---Departure
Thursday ,, 25	610	41.03	60.34	Wind W'ly (force 4), moderate breeze, slight sea, low swell; fine and clear
Friday ., 26	691	43.41	45.43	Wind W'ly (force 4), moderate breeze, moderate sea, low W'ly swell; mainly overcast and clear
Saturday ,, 27	679	47.50	30.38	Wind N.E. (force 4), moderate breeze, moderate sea, moderate swell; cloudy and clear
Sunday ,, 28	685	49.45	13.29	Wind N'ly (force 2), light breeze, slight sea, low swell; cloudy and clear
Monday ,, 29	461			At 0530 FT (0430 GMT) CH.1 buoy abeam— Arrival Cherbourg
Total	**3,126** nautical mile to Cherbourg			

PASSAGE—4 days, 10 hours, 6 minutes   **AVERAGE SPEED—29.46 knots**

REDUCED SPEED: 2 hours, 27 minutes

FASTEST EASTBOUND PASSAGE SINCE AUGUST, 1938

'The fastest eastbound passage since 1938', August 1966.

Toasting *QE2*, 20 September 1967.

During this voyage we had aboard a large number of press, radio and TV reporters and cameramen. We also had a fine model of the new ship aboard, taking it to New York. We docked at New York for the last time at 7.30 a.m. on 21 September 1967 having had quite a lot of fog the previous day and that night. This, of course, stops the captain's social activities as he is then always on the bridge. We had a very short stay there – twenty-eight hours to be exact – during which time much happened.

In 1967 our company relaxed its rule that captains' wives could not travel with them. Earlier in the year I had planned to take my wife to New York with me on 30 August, to leave her in America for a voyage, and then take her back on the sailing of 22 September. At the time the company had not announced that they were taking *Queen Mary* out of service in 1967. So, it was pure joss *(Chinese luck)* that I happened to have my wife with me for the final sailing from New York. This was a stroke of luck for us. My wife was there to greet me on arrival, having had a marvellous holiday with Mrs Bruce Merriman at Providence, Rhode Island and seen Bus Mosbacher win the Great Yacht Series there. She then stayed with Mrs Brewster Sewall and Miss Harriet Smith at Kennebunk, Maine. I held a final lunch party for some of my closest New York friends who had extended their generous hospitality to me over the years. My one regret was that I was not able to have my very good friends Mr and Mrs Hyme Ross and Mr Emmanuel Goldman to join me for lunch; they were always on Wall Street and 'GGG'. Missing also from this party was my pal, Bill Atherton who, for years had pleaded with me to bring my wife over, but when I did he regrettably departed from this world two days before she arrived; this was a sad blow to us. Nina, his wife, put on a brave face and came to my luncheon party.

My crew of course also had many friends in New York and they were somewhat peeved when we had a large Gala Dinner and Ball on board that night. We asked for volunteers, instead of the press-ganging them, and we had ample. This was really a magnificent final night for the *Queen Mary* at New York. This Ball was sponsored by the Travellers' Aid Society. My wife and I were guests and, for a change, I had the pleasure of sitting at a very famous Captain's Table aboard my own ship. The captain being none other than the great yacht skipper, Bus

Mosbacher. The guests at the ball included some of the most distinguished folks in the state of New York. I encountered many old friends and travellers that evening. It was a brilliant affair.

At 12.00 noon, Friday 22 September 1967, *Queen Mary* sailed for last time from New York. The piers were packed with people and we had a right-royal send off. Before sailing, there was a big press reception in the Smoke Room, where Mayor Lindsay made a moving farewell speech and presented me with a commemorative medallion. I was also presented with a commemorative plaque by the Navy League. It was with a feeling of sadness that I put the engines astern and backed out of Pier 92 for the last time. I wondered if I personally would ever see New York again as I was retiring along with the *Queen Mary*. I certainly hope to and meet my old friends again. Unfortunately, two of them, Mrs Hyme Ross and Mrs Jacob Larus have already departed from this world. New York will not be the same to me without them.

We were escorted out of harbour by a number of the Moran tugs who had aided us over the years with berthing. Normally we had six berthing and two leaving. The Manhattan Pleasure Boats were also out in force and packed, including the one my wife and I had toured Manhattan in a few weeks previously. Thereby hangs a little story. After leaving my wife in NY, she was riding in a taxi. The driver was chatty, as most NY taxi drivers are. In the course of the conversation he asked my wife if she had come over in the *Queen Mary*. When she replied yes, he said 'What do you think of that captain? He has been sailing to New York all these years and now he brought his wife here for the first time.' Before he could say anymore my wife thought that she better let him know that she was his wife, so said 'Well, I ought to be able to answer that question as I am his wife.' He was so amazed that he turned his head right round and said 'Gee, fancy that. What do you know? My wife will be excited to know I have been driving the captain of the *Queen Mary*'s wife' and with that, immediately ran into the back of the car ahead. He appeared to have a great kick out of driving my wife, so much so that he refused to take any fare from her – no taxi driver ever did likewise for me. My wife insisted he accept something and buy his wife a box of candy.

On this voyage there were many of my old table-friends travelling and this made it a little embarrassing as to who to invite to my table. I would have loved to have had them all but could only invite seven, and those were the seven who I first knew would be travelling. They were Mr and Mrs Condon, Mr and Mrs Ralston from Florida, Sir George and Lady Waller QC, and a great favourite of mine, Mrs Warren Webb from Philadelphia. The Ambrose Lighthouse gave us three blasts of its horn and dipped their ensign in reply to our farewell salutes and we were on our way in nice weather. We were fortunate and the weather was excellent all the way over.

I seldom entertained the first evening out and this was no exception. However, the next day the social whirl started in earnest. After my morning meeting with my Heads of Departments, I held a press conference at 10.15 a.m. and this was to be a daily event for this voyage. I always believed in giving the press any news of interest. This, I think, is good public relations and pays off, rather than saying nothing and letting them gather their information from any old source, half of which might not be correct. That evening I held a reception for all the First Class passengers in the Main Lounge and my wife received the guests with me. This reception was filmed by Paramount. For anyone who is not used to this, it is a bit of an ordeal under those powerful lights, and they are hot. My chief engineer who was also in the reception line was in a bath of perspiration; I am sure he was glad when they turned those lights off – so were we all for that matter. The following evening I held a reception for all the Cabin Class passengers and on that night, NBC did quite a bit of filming in the Dining Room. I never did see their film.

Thus it went on until we berthed at Cherbourg. Here we had another press reception, including the local press, and dignitaries. The Mayor of Cherbourg presented me with their medallion commemorating *Queen Mary*'s visits to their port.

Then, finally, our arrival at Southampton and the final press, radio and TV reception. We arrived at 5.30 p.m. It was 11 p.m. before I was able to leave and go home. By this time I was on my knees and ready to fall into my own bed. But it had all been exciting and the most interesting experience, which I was fortunate to have had.

On 27 September the Queen Mary *had completed her 1,000th and last crossing of the North Atlantic, having carried 2,112,000 passengers over 3,792,227 miles.*

In 1967 the *Queen Mary* was sold to the City of Long Beach, California, for the sum of US$3.45 million or £1.2 million. I was delighted. To have taken her to the scrapyard would have been a sacrilege. I was privileged and honoured to be her captain on her great final voyage. This was a most memorable cruise, the memories of which will, I am sure, remain with all of us who were privileged to be aboard, until the end of our days.

We sailed from Southampton at 9.30 a.m. on 31 October 1967, with 1,093 passengers and 806 crew, to the greatest farewell any ship has ever had. On the dockside was the immaculately dressed Royal Marine Band, in all their glorious colours, who played us away with inspiring music and finally to the tune of 'Auld Lang Syne'. The dockside and shores were bedecked with flags and deeply lined with people who had come from far and wide to bid us farewell. As we pulled off the quay, a squadron of naval helicopters flew over us in an anchor formation in final salute. As we slowly steamed out of harbour, flying the 310ft paying-off pennant, we were escorted by a fleet of small boats and our tugs. The ships in harbour said goodbye on their whistles and dipped their ensigns in salute, whilst many passed verbal 'goodbye and bon voyage' messages on their loud-hailer systems.

To me, the most moving farewell was that given us by the RMS *Oriana*. The crew of this very fine P&O passenger liner had lined their upper decks, all smartly dressed in their uniforms, and stood to attention as we passed, whilst their captain wished us 'farewell and good luck' over their loud-hailer. This was a real tribute from one fine ship, its captain and crew, to another and which we deeply appreciated.

On board one of our tugs, named the *Calshot*, were six retired *Queen Mary* captains and many high officials and dignitaries of the port and city of Southampton. Most of the captains said 'farewell and bon voyage' to me over the radio telephone.

All down the Solent, crowds of people lined the foreshores. After turning and passing Cowes, Isle of Wight, we increased speed and were then escorted through Portsmouth waters by two frigates of the Royal Navy. It was a sad moment when I slowed down the ship and said farewell to our pilot, Captain Jack Holt, who had piloted *Queen Mary* in and out of Southampton for many years. An excellent Pilot and real fine man who had a fund of good stories. I am sure he had as big a lump in his throat as he left as I did.

As we cleared the Solent and set course down the Channel we were met by HMS *Hermes*, an Aircraft Carrier of the Royal Navy, who had cleared the lower decks and manned their flight deck. As we steamed past her at full speed, they gave us three hearty cheers and wished us luck. The Royal Navy were certainly out in force to give us a great send-off that day.

Thus *Queen Mary* sailed from Southampton waters for the last time, bidding farewell to Britain forever, setting course down Channel for her new home, Long Beach, California. Many a tear was shed that day and there were many sad hearts in Britain as we disappeared over the horizon. It is really amazing the affection and feeling people can have for a ship; it was as if one were saying goodbye forever to a life-long love.

On board though, there was a new feeling of excitement and adventure stirring amongst the passengers and crew at the voyage ahead. This applied equally to me and my wife, Belle, who was sailing with me, courtesy of the City of Long Beach. She was my first (and only) mate, and what a fine mate she has been all our married life, and what an asset she proved to be on this voyage. On this voyage I would be visiting countries and sailing seas which were new to me, thus filling in the gaps in my world travels that remained after forty-six years at sea. I still need to visit New Zealand and then I can say I have visited every country with a coastline on the planet, except the Artic and Antarctic; and at this stage of my life I have no great desire to visit the latter two. This, the final voyage of my seagoing career, gave me the opportunity of becoming a 'Cape Horner', and steaming up the west coast of South America

HMS *Hermes* bids farewell to the *Queen Mary*, with the crew lining the side.

and visiting Chile and Peru for the first time. If I had been given the choice, I could not have chosen a more exciting voyage to end my career.

Some of the background problems during the final cruise will be of interest.

The *Queen Mary* was, at that time, the second largest passenger liner ever built, having a gross tonnage of 81,237 tons; the only ship larger was the *Queen Elizabeth* at 83,673 tons. Her length is 1,019½ft; breadth 118ft and when loaded there was 39½ft under the water, which is known as the draft of a vessel.

Due to her size, it was not possible to take her through the Panama Canal to Long Beach, so we had to take her via Cape Horn. It would have been just possible to take her through the Straits of Magellan, thus saving 200 miles, but this is a dangerous, rocky, poorly lighted passage with tricky approaches. The risk was too big for a ship of this size, so round Cape Horn it was to be. After all, we all wanted to call ourselves 'Cape Horners' as that was part of the attraction of the cruise. In the contract Cunard would have paid about US$800,000 to take her round with a skeleton crew, but the City also had the option of putting passengers in it if they so wished. They exercised this option against Cunard's advice. The main reason being that *Queen Mary* was not suited for passengers in tropical weather, the ship not being air conditioned. The responsibility of booking passengers was given to Furgazy, an American travel agency.

There were many problems to face taking *Queen Mary* these 25,000 miles on that particular route. The two major ones being: refuelling and obtaining fresh water in the quantities we would require to cope with the needs of two thousand people and twenty-four thirsty boilers. At full speed, with all engines and boilers, *Queen Mary* used 1,100 tons of oil fuel per day to do 29 knots; this is 1.6 tons of oil fuel per mile. We had storage for 7,500 tons. We always allowed for a safety margin of 1½ days steaming, so this meant we could only go six days without refuelling. Fuel was no problem as far as Rio de Janeiro, but, after Rio we could not obtain any worthwhile supply until Balboa, at the western end of the Panama Canal; this being 7,000 miles, it meant that we could not make it at full speed. We also used 200 tons a day of fresh water for the boilers and 3,000 people used, for domestic purposes 600 tons each day, making a total of 800 tons per day of fresh water. After leaving Las Palmas, in the Canary Islands, we would be unable to go alongside in any port until we reached Balboa, and it was found that no ports en-route could supply us with that amount of water. To overcome these two constraints and thus be able to take passengers, it was decided to use only two out of the four engines and half the boilers. This would cut down the oil consumption to 550 tons per day, instead of 1,100, and also save 100 tons of water a day on boilers. We could then almost halve the Engine and Boiler Room personnel.

Over the years, statistics showed that we used one ton of fresh water per day for every five persons aboard, so if we could reduce the personnel, we would not require as much fresh water. To do this we used only two dining rooms, one for the passengers and one for the crew, using the same kitchen and kitchen staff for both. We closed down all crew mess-rooms and the tourist dining room and kitchen. By these means we were able to reduce the crew from 1,050 to 806 without the service suffering, other than that there were two sittings in the Dining Room. Thus, we were able to reduce the fresh water per day to a maximum of 550 tons and, at this figure, the water problem was solved.

Queen Mary had never steamed on two engines before. It was estimated that she would be able to do 22½ knots with the two. The cruise was scheduled on this, but it later proved that we were unable to do more than 21½ knots. When I discovered this, I found that we could not keep to the original schedule and it was therefore necessary to revise the schedule.

I am afraid the cruise did not get off to a good start. We ran into a south-westerly gale the first night out. This, unfortunately, put something of a damper on people's spirits, with many feeling the effects of the ship's motion. Even ships of this size can pitch and roll when seas are high, and, so far, nothing has been invented to stop or ease the pitching motion, although stabilisers have succeeded in cutting down the roll to a minimum. This affected our entertainers as well and I well remember Johnny Mathis valiantly trying to do his stuff, but I am afraid he did not look as if he was enjoying it and was unable to give of his best.

The gale also reduced our speed, sufficiently to cause me to miss the scheduled tide at Lisbon and thus had to wait twelve hours for the next high water. There is not sufficient water on the bar at our draft to cross it except at high water, and even then there was only 3ft to spare. Here also there is often a heavy swell running which makes it even worse and, if big enough, could make it impossible. This day there was quite a swell running after the gale. Though there is plenty of water in the river, inside the bar, at any state of the tide, there was not sufficient water alongside any of the piers for us to berth alongside; so we had to anchor off in the river and the passengers were ferried ashore in local ferries which we hired.

We stayed in Lisbon for a bare twenty-four hours, but this gave us enough time for everyone to do a tour or two and have a quick look at the beautiful city and surrounding country, as well as the many places of interest. I managed to take a few hours off and take my wife ashore to meet some Welsh friends of ours from our home town and do a tour of some of the interesting places. Whilst at one of these, I noticed that time was ticking along and, as I was sailing at 3.00 p.m., I wanted to be aboard at least one hour before sailing. I said to our party that we must be heading back. One of my passengers overheard me and said 'There is no need to hurry. I know the captain will not sail before 3 o'clock.' The lady with him looked at me and suddenly recognised me as the captain, and told him that it is the captain you have spoken to. Was his face red; we all had a big laugh though.

When discussing the entertainment for the cruise, I refused to hold any receptions until after Lisbon due to the possibility of bad weather before then. I think everyone eventually was glad that I had done so, though much pressure had been put on me to start as soon as we left Southampton. After Lisbon the cruise really got under way and the social whirl started. That night I held my first reception and during the next two evenings Belle and I met and shook hands with the 1,100 passengers. It was a pleasure to meet them all and especially to see all the ladies in their beautiful evening gowns. Contrary to what people think, I have always enjoyed meeting people and entertaining. Many people have said to me over the years 'You must be bored with it all'. But, I ask you, what man could grow bored of meeting so many beautiful ladies and so many interesting men, certainly not me.

The Captain's Table, during the farewell voyages, 1967.

The receptions set everyone off. The 'ice was broken' as the saying goes, but really there was no ice to break. Everyone started to enjoy the sun and good weather, and let their hair down. When we sailed into the tropics, they needed to let more than that down to cool off.

It was only during this passage to Las Palmas that I began to realise that we were not going to be able to get 22½ knots on the two engines. I gave her a further test after leaving there and found that 21½ knots was our maximum speed. This rather upset the applecart a bit when I informed everyone at my daily morning meeting of my Heads of Departments and the Long Beach and Furgazy representatives. We therefore worked out a new schedule, based on the overriding factor that we must arrive in Long Beach by 10.00 hrs on 9 December. This meant curtailing our time in some of the intermediate ports, Valparaiso, Callao, Balboa and Acapulco. Except for one or two people, the passengers took it in good part. The odd one or two felt they were being done out of something, and one particular gentleman voiced the opinion that he did not consider it safe for a ship of this size to steam on two engines at 22 knots when she was designed to steam on four engines at 30 – some people have strange ideas. Our policy in Cunard had always been to try and please 100 per cent of our passengers. If we succeed in pleasing 95 per cent, we consider we have done well. As time has proved, that in any walk of life, with the transport and hotel business in particular, it is impossible to please everyone, no matter how hard one tries.

One of the other problems we had to face was the heat. *Queen Mary* was designed and built especially for the North Atlantic trade. She was well ahead of her time in having air-conditioning in the First Class public rooms. In those days there were not many ships trading in the tropics that had any air-conditioning. She certainly was not designed for the tropics and we knew she would be uncomfortably hot there, as she used to be in midsummer in New York. At all my first receptions it was always my policy to say a few words of welcome to my passengers and hope they would enjoy themselves; on this voyage I told them of the problems we had to face, that the ship would become very hot as she was not conditioned, but that we would do everything possible to keep her as cool as we could. Also that, due to the difficulty in obtaining fresh water, I asked them not to waste it. The response was remarkable, no one complained of the heat and the water consumption was well below the average. We had plenty of liquor and ice, but they did not swim or bath in it; maybe they did not drink water for a change!

Whilst at Rio de Janeiro we had to fill right up with fresh water and take on a large amount of fuel oil. This meant that we had small, antiquated craft alongside the ship all the time we were pumping oil and water. It did not help that most of them seemed to be coal burners which belched out smoke and steam the whole time. It was therefore necessary to keep the portholes closed day and night, if not you were smoked or steamed out of your cabin, as some passengers and crew found out. This actually happened to passengers in the best suite of rooms, but they took it well, bless them.

During the worst of the heat I used to take Belle with me to have a chat with the men in the kitchens and see what their conditions were like. They were really working under almost unbearable conditions, temperatures reaching as high as 120°F *(49°C)*. Yet they did not complain but laughed and shrugged it off. They were a remarkably good crew. They worked hard and well for thirty-nine days and at least fourteen hours a day, without a day off in all that time. In port during normal cruising they would expect a little let up, especially the cooks and stewards, but there was none. In fact, the pressure was even greater in port as we had to cater for such large numbers of official guests to cocktail and dinner parties. This was the straw that nearly broke the camel's back. Towards the end of cruise I had one occasion when I had to talk to some of my stewards, give them a pat on the back and persuade them to keep going and not let the side down, as there was only a couple of days to go and it would be all over. They were showing signs of exhaustion and perhaps breaking under the strain; however they kept going. Not many crews would have worked like these boys did on that cruise, especially since quite a lot of them knew that they had no jobs to go to after they returned to England. This was real loyalty and devotion to duty. I was very proud of them all.

But, enough of the problems – now a little about the amusing and entertaining points of the cruise.

Just prior to sailing, for publicity purposes, I was photographed with some of the beautiful hostesses employed by Furgazy. During the voyage these were on display with lots of other photographs taken by the ship's photographer, on the promenade deck. One day, Belle, my wife was looking at these and next to her were a couple of ladies doing likewise. They obviously spotted this photograph of me with these girls. One said to the other 'Gee, he isn't a bad looking fella, but I do not think I would like to be married to him though. I wonder what he is like to live with and what his wife would think if she saw him with these girls.' They turned to my wife and said 'How would you like to be married to him?' My wife never did tell me what reply she gave them, or if she ever told them that she was married to me.

Another amusing, but somewhat embarrassing, incident occurred when Belle and I were walking the promenade deck one forenoon. When saying good morning to my passengers on meeting, I have always liked, when possible, to address them by name. There was a lady walking towards us, Belle, I thought said to me 'This is Mrs Crotchety coming along.' So when we came up to her I gave her a salute and said 'Good morning Mrs Crotchety' and stopped and had a chat with her. After we parted, Belle burst out laughing. I asked her what she was laughing about; she replied 'That is not that lady's name. I said this lady coming along is rather crotchety.' The word 'crotchety' in Britain means inclined to complain about everything, to be dissatisfied and not happy about things. Was my face red! The lady, fortunately, did not realise what I had said or, if she did, did not wish to embarrass me. If the lady in question ever hears this little story, I trust she will forgive Belle and me, and have a good laugh at my expense.

In a speech he recalls that, after a reception given by the British Ambassador in Rio de Janeiro, he and Belle were driven back to Queen Mary *in his official Rolls-Royce, flying the Royal Standard, probably the first time this had ever happened to a liner captain and his wife.*

The two Captains, during the farewell voyages, 1967.

During this cruise we had two modern and recently built bridges to pass under: one at Lisbon and one at Balboa. The former was no problem as we had passed under it before, but the ship had never been to Balboa before and this bridge had been fairly recently completed. Cunard marine advisors, who carefully investigate beforehand the ports it is intended for us to call at, informed me that there was sufficient clearance for me to pass under this bridge, though we were not given the height of it.

Some days before I was due to arrive there, I received a message from the Harbour Master to the effect that he had been given a different height of our masts by Cunard New York, and, if it was correct, we would not be able to pass under the bridge. Would I confirm the height of my masts; this I could confirm as 237ft from keel to masthead and that my draft would be around 35ft; thus from the waterline it would be 202ft. I asked him to give me height of his bridge above high water mark – I never did have a reply. Though I was in no real doubt about it, at the next port I sent my men up the masts and had them remove the 4ft weather vanes from the top that had been there for thirty years. When the Balboa Pilot and Harbour Master boarded, they were still rather nervous about the clearance under the bridge. They then told me the height of their bridge and I assured them we could pass under, but the Pilot still seemed rather worried, so we passed under the bridge at half tide. As we approached the bridge, one of the wags amongst the passengers started to take bets as to whether we could get under or not. Entering into the fun of it, I spoke to the passengers on the foredeck over the load-hailer and said 'You see those people standing on the centre of the bridge. If you see them suddenly start to run, you better do so also as you will then know we are not going to make it.' The people on the bridge stood their ground, so did my passengers. We passed safely underneath with about 5ft between the bridge and my mast, and about 3ft of water under my keel. Looking from down below, it always looks as if we must hit the bridge; this is, of course, an optical illusion, due to the angle of sight. We were piloted in by Capt. Hay, a man of vast experience, assisted by Mr Lyons. I was deeply grieved to hear later that Capt. Hay died of a heart attack a week or two later.

One evening towards the end of the cruise a lady passenger stopped one of my young officers and said 'Young man, I have enjoyed the cruise, but I have been ill in bed for a week. During that time I had the most comfortable bedpan I have ever had the occasion to use. Do you think I could buy it and if so, do you think the captain would autograph it for me?' I never received an official request to do so. I must presume that she did not succeed in buying it before arriving at Long Beach, or that no one had the nerve to ask me to autograph it. I have autographed some peculiar things in my time – but a bedpan? Perhaps she was successful at

John and Belle, during the final voyage in 1967.

the sale of *Queen Mary* bits and pieces later at Long Beach. For her sake, I trust that she has had no occasion to need one since.

I suppose the real highlight of the cruise was the rounding of Cape Horn. Very few of us aboard had ever done this before – certainly I never had. Most of us had read, at some time or other, about the bad weather that used to haunt the sailing ships in the days gone by. The great difficulty they had in sailing west round it was due to the persistent westerly gales and the east flowing currents. Many ships gave it up, turned round and went east to Australia and many were lost there with all hands.

Our highlight turned out to be somewhat flat. Instead of the westerly gales everyone expected us to have, what did we, the biggest ship ever to go round it get? What the sailing ship captains prayed for and seldom were granted – a moderate north–east breeze with a moderate little sea. It was Sunday 19 November 1967. There was a little light misty rain early on which cleared away by noon and the sun came out to give us a very pleasant mild afternoon, with the temperature of 40°F *(4°C)*. Everyone was looking forward excitedly to seeing the Horn. We expected to pass it somewhere round 3 p.m. A sweep was run by the entertainment staff as to the exact minute we would have it bearing due north; this was well patronised.

On board we had two red London buses which the City of Long Beach had purchased in England and which I had stowed on deck, on the after end of the ship. To raise some funds for the needy children of Valparaiso, sister city to Long Beach, the city officials advertised a little gimmick – round Cape Horn in a London bus and have your photograph taken with the Cape in the background. This was very popular and quite a number of dollars were raised in this way. Some decide to cycle round and did so on the cycles in the gym. Others said that they swam round – in the pool. We actually passed Cape Horn at 3.01 p.m. at a distance of 1¼ miles, with the sun shining. The Horn had a mantle of cloud on the top, like a headdress. Visibility was excellent and we could see the snow capped mountains in the distance. There was no sign of the fire which gives this land the name *Tierra del Fuego*. It is very barren, rocky country. We saw no signs of life and even the lighthouse structure was difficult to pick out, even at a mile. No wonder ships of old treated it with such awe and gave it a wide berth.

After returning to England, I was invited to the Cape Horners' annual dinner in London and there met Sir Alec Rose who sailed single-handed around the world via Cape Horn. He told me he had purposely kept well clear of it and not even seen it. As you may be aware, the trend in recent years has been to sail the smallest craft, single-handed around the world and Cape Horn. These achievements have been rewarded with due recognition such as knighthoods, etc. This was something very different; this was the largest ship ever to round Cape Horn.

Rounding
Cape Horn.

As she was flying the British flag, 'our Harold', the Prime Minister, decided that he must
do something about this, and so called his pals around him; 'We must to do something to
commemorate this great occasion' says he to them. After a long and secret meeting, they
thought of a brilliant idea which would make the whole world remember this date – they
decided to devalue the Pound Sterling. Of course they said that it was to help the British
financial situation and exports, but I and my crew knew it was to commemorate the day
Queen Mary rounded Cape Horn and also to make sure we did not have so many dollars to
spend when we arrived at Long Beach. *The socialist Harold Wilson was not one of John's favourite
politicians!* We shall always remember that day, its excitement, its joys – and devaluation!

By midnight it was blowing a north-westerly gale, so the Horn did not let us off scot-free.
I suspect that this pleased those passengers who were good sailors. We had a Cape Horn
reception that evening to celebrate; the caviar and champagne flowed freely; a night to
remember, but not like the movie.

Mayor and Mrs Wade had a surprise packet by which to remember the Horn. A seagull flew
in through their porthole in the early hours of the morning. This rather startled them as well
as the bedroom steward who had the job of catching it and returning form whence it came.
In the process, the gull decided he was not going to leave hungry, so had a bite of Cunard
steward for breakfast – Cunard, living up to its name of never allowing a guest or passenger,
even a stowaway, to depart hungry. I heard that a press statement stated that a dead seagull had
been put in Mayor Wade's cabin by one of the crew; if so, this was completely untrue.

This is the first time I have heard of a gull entering through a porthole, though many
do land on board and rest. I know of flying-fish flying into cabins; I remember during my
apprenticeship days, one flying slap through the mosquito gauze in the porthole of the
captain's cabin and landing in bed with him. I believe it was a female one and a tasty dish
for the captain's breakfast. We apprentices used to search the foredeck at first light for any
flying-fish that may have come aboard, attracted by the light, during the night. This frequently
happened in the tropics; fresh fish was a luxury for us in those days. *He recalls a dinner with the
President of Peru at Callao, with its contrasting great poverty and wealth.*

Of all the ports we visited I personally think that Acapulco has the most beautiful setting
with its almost land-locked hills and colourful houses. Excepting Long Beach, this is the only
port that really gave us a welcome, not with a fleet of boats afloat, but with what they laid
on ashore at the landing place. There was an official reception on the landing for the Mayor
and his lady and my wife and me. Gifts were exchanged by Mayor Wade for Long Beach and
the local mayor; I was presented with a beautiful silver cigarette box. Mexican dancers and
orchestras entertained in their colourful costumes with beautiful young dancers who danced
gracefully; it was a pleasure to watch and listen to them. Free drinks were being dispensed,

On the final voyage.

apparently for all and sundry, or at least it seemed so. We were then whisked away by the Director of the Mexican Tourist Bureau to see the sights of Acapulco. The highlight of this trip was a visit to the President's summer house in the hills on the eastern shore of the bay from where the *Queen Mary* seemed like a toy floating on a lake. A most unusual sight in the harbour was a London Barge converted into a yacht, flying the British ensign; the owner invited me aboard but, regretfully, time did not permit me to accept or reciprocate.

This was our last port of call before we reached Long Beach. As we would have quite an appreciable amount of food left over on arrival at LB, it was suggested that we landed it at Acapulco for use of the needy, as US regulations forbade it being landed in the USA. Mayor

Wade and his officials looked into this, but again time and restrictions did not permit. All this food was, I believe, eventually put into barges, towed out to sea and dumped – such a terrible waste!

Now came our final passage from Acapulco to Long Beach. A big press contingent boarded at Acapulco and was with us on this final leg. Much has been said and printed of this final passage and the terrific welcome at Long Beach. Amongst my many fond memories, it was marked by two outstanding events.

The first was the dropping of flowers on board from a jet plane on the day before arrival. This was something out of the usual and created quite a lot of excitement on board. After two or three dummy-runs, the plane released its flowers about a quarter mile ahead of the ship at a height of about 300ft. It was successful and many of the flowers landed aboard. This was to emulate the story that Eddie Rickenbacker flew over the *Queen Mary* on her maiden arrival at New York, however, I understand that Eddie Rickenbacker stated that there is no truth to this story.

Secondly, there was our farewell cocktail party. The ship still had a very ample supply of champagne and liquor remaining, so this flowed very freely, with everyone doing their utmost to reduce the stock remaining, yet despite all their valiant effort, we still had quite a lot of stock left on arrival. There was also a good supply of Havana cigars in hand; these we issued liberally to the guests that evening as it was illegal to land Havana cigars in the USA. Never have so many cigars been smoked in such a short space of time by so few. The Final Ball that night was, without doubt, the biggest 'gala' held on *Queen Mary* since her Maiden Voyage in 1936, although the final one on the Atlantic back in September took some surpassing. Underneath though, there was a feeling of sadness, especially amongst the crew, as this was the last ball ever to be held aboard *Queen Mary* at sea. There will doubtless be many such fine occasions again on board, but not at sea where one can feel the hum of the engines and motors with the slight vibrations that seem to bring the ship to life.

Then came the dawn of that never to be forgotten day, 9 December 1967, when the *Queen Mary* arrived at Long Beach. This was the day all California and, in particular, Long Beach had been waiting for. This day they were all out on the cliffs, hilltops, beaches and the water to greet 'Their *Queen Mary*'. Mayor Wade had asked me very early on in the voyage if I would arrive at daylight off Newport Beach and proceed as close inshore as possible to the eastern end of Long Beach breakwater and then proceed as far west as Firmin Point before picking up my Pilot and entering harbour. This I did, keeping just outside the ten fathom line up to Long Beach, then half a mile off the breakwater. Shortly after 7 a.m. we were off Newport Beach and were met by a Great Armada of boats of all sorts, shapes and sizes. Unfortunately the wind suddenly sprang up to gale-force and made things somewhat uncomfortable for our welcomers in the small craft who found difficulty in trying to keep up with us. Though I quickly reduced revolutions to 8 knots from Newport, a ship of this size carries her way for quite a distance. The gale-force winds did not last long but the wind still remained strong for the final approach. I am quite sure that no ship has ever had such a reception as *Queen Mary* did that day at Long Beach. Never have I seen so many craft on the water at the same time and covering such an area. One had to be there to believe it. It was estimated that there were four to five thousand craft in all; all well disciplined and behaved. What a sight they were and not one caused me any moment of anxiety. Thanks to all of them and the efficiency of the Coast Guards who made perfect sheepdogs. The US Navy was not to be outdone and also had their Nuclear Cruiser *Long Beach* out there to greet us.

At 9.56 a.m. I stopped and Pilots Jacobsen and Aultman boarded and at 10.22 a.m. we entered the breakwater and headed for our berth. The Pilots and tugs did such a fine job that at 11.30 a.m. we were secured in berth. The tugs assisting us were *Sea Otter, Rival, Escort, Long Beach* and *Terminal Island* – my thanks to the captains of them all.

At 12.07 p.m. I personally put the telegraphs to 'Finish with Engines'. The *Queen Mary's* engines had turned for the last time; the shafts were then disconnected from the engines and the ship was made immobile.

Queen Mary arriving at Long Beach.

As soon as the gangway was aboard, Mayor Wade and I met at the top of it and proceeded ashore. We were met at the bottom by Vice-Mayor Robert Crowe who was immaculately dressed in a grey suit, bowler hat and rolled umbrella; he could have been taken for a London business executive. Much to my amusement, Mayor Wade came ashore with one of our sailor's round hats with the Cunard ribbon on his head. Our wives followed us and we were escorted and led by the colourful and smartly dressed Marine Flag Bearers to the reception rostrum, where my wife and I formally met the City Councillors and Officials. We were presented with a huge key to the city made of lovely flowers; it was very beautiful.

Thus ended the Final Voyage of *Queen Mary* and my own sea-going career. It was a very sad moment when I signed her over to the City of Long Beach at noon on 11 December 1967 in a very colourful ceremony on the after-end of the Boat Deck. This was finalised by the hauling down of the British Ensign and Cunard House Flags and hoisting in their place the flags of the United States and the City of Long Beach. For a moment I was unable to control my feelings and shed a few tears on *Queen Mary*'s deck. *Having taken his previous command, the* Mauretania, *to the scrap-yard John was delighted that Long Beach had bought* Queen Mary

The City of Long Beach gave my wife and me a magnificent reception and we thoroughly enjoyed the great and varied hospitality extended to us during our week in Long Beach. We were especially grateful to Mr Howard Eggerton for personally piloting us in his own helicopter over Long Beach, Los Angeles, Hollywood and Beverly Hills. This really gave us a bird's-eye view of that part of California, and it certainly looked good from the air. I have to admit though that the motion almost made me sick for a while whilst my wife was quite unperturbed.

The moment of the sale of *Queen Mary*.

For the biggest thrill I am indebted to Mr William Bergen for inviting us to lunch at the Space Division of Rockwell Corporation. He introduced us to his team of space experts who showed us slides and explained how it was planned to land men on the moon. During the tour I was very privileged to be allowed to sit, or rather lay, in the captain's position in the command module of Apollo 8, which had been in space and recovered just a month or so previously, and also to have their experts explain some of the intricate instruments. We were then taken through and shown the factory where they were making and assembling command and service modules for the future moon shots. Belle and I found it all completely fascinating and it was a great event for us.

Since I delivered the *Queen Mary* to Long Beach I have not taken another ship to sea, retiring from The Cunard Line on 31 August 1968.

⇌ ⇌ ⇌

An interesting postscript is told by David Hutchings in his book on the Caronia:

In early 1968 the Caronia *lay alongside Berth 101, the traditional lay-up berth in Southampton, awaiting a buyer. In readiness for her sale she was to be dry-docked for the last time in Southampton. She was commanded for this short trip from Berth 101 to No. 6 Dry Dock by Captain John Treasure Jones.*

This would be the only time that Captain Treasure Jones would have the Caronia *under his command (although he was the staff captain for the 1954/55 World Cruise). He would say years later that, because he loved the* Mauretania, *and Captain 'Bill' Warwick loved the* Caronia, *they had come to a mutual agreement not to 'swap' ships, as was the custom, but retain their own beloved commands. As result, Captain Warwick became the only captain to take the* Caronia *('my yacht' as he liked to describe her) on two world cruises.*

Retiring at age 63, he had, apart from three years ashore during the depression, served almost 43½ continuous years at sea. In an interview with David Hutchings he summed up his rules of thumb which kept him out of trouble:

> *Never rely on a Pilot. Always be one step ahead of him.*
> *Get everything down in writing if the situation warrants it.*
> *Never take risks that you can't see the outcome of.*
> *Always enjoy the difficult challenge.*

CHAPTER 7

PERSONAL NOTES
AND THE EPILOGUE

In November 1964 I was elected a Member of the Honourable Company of Master Mariners, whose headquarters are in *Wellington*, a ship I commanded during the war.

On the Final Voyage of *Queen Mary* in 1967 I was made an Honorary Member of the Panama Canal Pilots Association and at Long Beach I have had the following honours bestowed on me:

Honorary Pilot of the Port of Long Beach

Honorary Life Member of Long Beach Chamber of Commerce

Honorary Member of Long Beach Yacht Club

First Honorary Member of *Queen Mary* Club of the Chamber of Commerce Long Beach

Honorary Commodore of *Queen Mary* Club of the Chamber of Commerce, Long Beach

The First Honorary Port Ambassador of the Port of Long Beach

I was presented with a Plaque of Appreciation by the Rotary Club of the City of Long Beach.

In 1968 I was honoured by the University of Wales when, at a ceremony at Cardiff, His Royal Highness Prince Phillip, The Duke of Edinburgh, conferred on me an Honorary Degree of Doctor of Law.

I am an Honorary Rotarian of Haverfordwest Rotary Club and, some years ago, was granted the Freedom of my home town, Haverfordwest, an honour I much appreciated.

Up until 1965 the family resided in Haverfordwest, Pembrokeshire. Even today it takes quite a time to commute between Haverfordwest and Liverpool or Southampton. Upon taking command of Queen Mary, *with the short turn-rounds in Southampton, it was decided that this location would be a much more convenient home base. They then moved to Chandlers Ford, between Southampton and Winchester.*

My hobbies, when I have the time, are gardening and golf; my handicap in the latter being fourteen. *John was member at Haverfordwest Golf Club, followed by Stoneham Golf Club, in Southampton. Indeed, he played his usual eighteen holes only a few days before his sudden death, aged almost eighty-eight years old. He regularly played cricket for the Master Mariners Cricket Club until he was eighty-three. He was a member of the Royal Southampton Yacht Club. He could also play the piano and the mandolin.*

≈≈≈

John had married 'Belle' on 30 August 1933. As the Great Depression had started to bite, he had been laid off by White Star Line at the end of October 1931, and returned home to work on his father's farm outside Haverfordwest. As a twenty-six year old, fancy-free young man of the world, he obviously had not 'let the grass grow under his feet' and had been busy courting. Her father was an influential man in the community as the Secretary General of the National Farmers Union in West Wales. Born on 18 November 1909, she was baptised Eulalie Isobel Lees, named apparently by her French nanny. John's private nickname for her at home was 'Tops'.

John and Belle had four children:

Michael, born 23 July 1942, whilst John was on convoy duty with HMS Sunflower;

David, born 28 February 1946, whilst he was in Indonesia;

Susan, born 7 December 1947, whilst he was away on MV Britannic;

Robert, born 30 September 1952, whilst he was away on RMS Queen Elizabeth.

Doctor of Law investiture.

Life has always been tough for the wives of seafarers!

Looking through the records in his 'Certificate of Discharge' books one notes that he was only home for Christmas in 1951 and '65 during the post-war years. The story is told in the family how, one afternoon around 1950, two of the children were looking out of the front window of the house and saw a man with a suitcase walking up the road. 'Do you know who that is?' asked Michael. 'No' replied the young Susan, shaking her head; 'that's our father' was his response.

On Tuesday, 16 July 1968, Susan was married at the seafarer's church, St Mary's in Southampton, which was followed by the reception on board the Queen Elizabeth *alongside the Ocean Terminal. Being a unique occasion, it was widely covered in the national press and by the BBC. Over the years John had received much hospitality from his many friends in the United States so he was particularly pleased to be able to make a token return of this by inviting some of them as guests to the wedding.*

David, at fifteen, had some ideas of following his father to sea. So, in March 1961, he was sent off on a trip to New York on the Queen Mary *returning on the* Queen Elizabeth. *John was then the captain of the* Saxonia *and was able to spend a few days with him in New York. Following his experience of the North Atlantic at this time of the year, he decided to become an accountant. Susan and her husband made the historic and memorable Maiden Crossing of QM2 to New York in April 2004.*

Susan's wedding – alongside the *Queen Elizabeth*.

Susan's wedding – on the bridge.

John and Belle, 1966.

In her later years Belle was laid low with Alzheimer's. Undaunted, John took over all of her care and the running of house. He became a competent cook and many of those who called at the house particularly remembered his great skill in baking scones and cakes. As David Hutchings recalls:

> *On more than one occasion he has cut a 'phone call short with the news that his latest batch of strawberry jam was just reaching its critical point and that he would 'phone back later! This jam would duly be fed to visitors along with homemade cake or scones.*

John died suddenly of an aneurism on Tuesday 18 May 1993, just three months short of his eighty-eighth birthday.

In a tribute, David Hutchings wrote, 'the funeral on 19 May was blessed with a beautifully sunny English spring afternoon, with a balmy breeze blowing in from the Channel.'

The service was held at St Mary's, the parish church of nearby Otterbourne. Amongst the mourners were at least four retired Cunard captains, Heier, Jackson, Portet and Warwick, as well as several other captains (retired) from Southampton Master Mariners. At 2.30 p.m. the coffin, covered in the Blue Ensign of the RNR and surmounted by the captain's sword, cap and medals, was borne into the church on the shoulders of the pall bearers. The service was conducted by the parish priest and by the Canon of the Mission to Seafarers, who read the eulogy. The interment was at the Chandlers Ford cemetery

Belle passed away eleven days after John and was buried a week to the day after him.

1 The *Queen Mary* on her sea trials in the Clyde. (JCM)

2 Colour image of the *Normandie*, *Queen Mary*'s arch-rival, from *L'Illustration*. (JCM)

3 *Lancastria* (served on during 1937-38).

4 *Laurentic* (served on during 1939-40).

5 *Samaria* (served on during 1947–51).

6 *Scythia* (served on during 1947).

7 *Georgic* and *Britannic*. (© Stephen J. Card)

8 *Ascania* (served on during 1950-51).

9 *Caronia* – 'The Green Goddess' (served on during 1954-57).

10 *Queen Mary* (served on during 1953-67).

11 *Queen Elizabeth* (served on during 1948-65).

Opposite: 12 *Media* (served on during 1957-59). On a south-westerly course, outbound from Liverpool for New York, she is passing the South Stack Lighthouse off Holy Island, Anglesey, North Wales. This picture was painted from an account of a voyage undertaken by Kenneth Vard at which time Captain Treasure Jones was in command. (© Kenneth Vard & Stephen J. Card)

13 *Sylvania* (served on during 1959).

14 *Saxonia* (served on during 1959-62).

Opposite: 15 *Mauretania*, 1939. In this painting the beautiful new *Mauretania* enters New York harbour at the end of her maiden voyage. She is escorted by the Moran tugs and the new liner *Panama* is about to pass to starboard. (© Kenneth Vard & Stephen J. Card)

16 *Mauretania*, 1964. In October 1962, while the *Mauretania* was in Southampton for her annual refit, she was painted in the line's pale green cruising livery. Here she is painted as outbound from Southampton at the start of a cruise to the Norwegian fjords and North Cape. (© Stephen J. Card)

17 *Mauretania*
– classic livery.

18 *Mauretania*
– white livery.

19 *Mauretania*
– green livery. (JCM)

20 *Mauretania* (served on during 1939–1965). Described as 'an extraordinarily fine ship' which remained 'a happy ship' to the end, she is painted here, as many would like her to be remembered, outbound from New York in the winter of 1947–48 at the start of a Caribbean cruise. (© Stephen J. Card)

21 *Queen Mary*. (© Stephen J. Card)

22 *Queen Mary* at speed. This painting is one of Stephen's favourites. From our vantage point on *Queen Elizabeth's* Boat Deck, we see the powerful *Queen Mary* as she steams past, homeward bound for Southampton, her stem buried in an oncoming swell. With her long, low profile topped by three perfectly proportioned funnels, she looks the ultimate ocean greyhound. (© Stephen J. Card)

Previous page: 23 *Queen Mary* – The Final Farewell. From her main mast she flies her enormous paying-off pennant. This red, white and blue ribbon was 310ft long – 10ft for every year of service. She is dressed overall and smoke streams from her enormous orange-red funnels. The skyscrapers of Manhattan are receding in the background as the ship points her bows eastwards for the last time. (© Kenneth Vard & Derrick Smooth)

24 Captain, *Queen Mary*, 1967.

Right: 25 Freedom of Haverfordwest,
1978. The photograph shows John
receiving his charter as a Burgess, from
Lt-Col. J.H.V. Higgon OBE, DL, JP,
Master of the Guild, on 11 July 1978.

Below: 26 The Queen Mother, 1986.

Above left: 27 *Queen Mary* poster. (JCM)

Above right: 28 *Queen Mary* publicity material. (JCM)

Left: 29 The Hailes Trophy, or Blue Riband. (JCM)

30 The Cabin Smoking Room, *Queen Mary*. (JCM)

CHURCHMAN'S CIGARETTES

THE "QUEEN MARY"; FITTING ONE OF THE 4 PROPELLERS

CHURCHMAN'S CIGARETTES

THE "QUEEN MARY"; FRAMEWORK OF BOWS WITH STEM IN POSITION

Left and far left: 31 and 32 Part of a series of cigarette cards issued at the time of launching the *Queen Mary*. (JCM)

Below: 33 Postcard from the early twentieth century depicting Cunard's sister ships together. (JCM)

CUNARD'S WONDER SHIPS

Queen Elizabeth   *Queen Mary*

BY FAR THE LARGEST SUPERLINERS IN THE WORLD

SALUTE to R.M.S. "QUEEN ELIZABETH"
(the world's largest liner)
HOMEWARD BOUND FROM NEW YORK ON HER
last Transatlantic Crossing to Southampton via Cherbourg
WEDNESDAY, OCTOBER 30 to MONDAY, NOVEMBER 4, 1968

34 The *Queen Elizabeth* homeward-bound from New York in 1968. (JCM)

5 The *Queen Elizabeth*'s luxurious main lounge. (JCM)

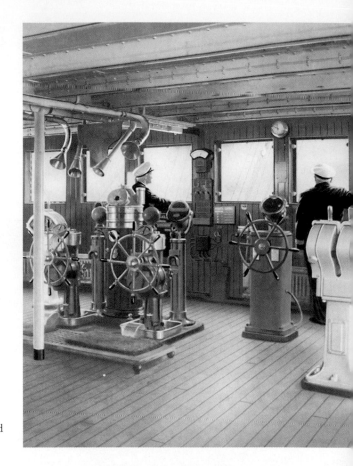

Right: 36 The Bridge on the *Queen Elizabeth.* (JCM)

Below: 37 In an effort to make them pay through the Depression ships like *Britannic* and *Franconia* were sent cruising. (JCM)

38 The interior of a boiler-room. (JCM)

39 RMS *Mauretania*, the world's fastest liner for over twenty years. (JCM)

40 Charles Pear's painting of RMS *Mauretania* coming under the Forth Bridge on her way to the breaker's yard. (JCM)

41 A Cunarder unloading cargo in London Docks. (JCM)

42 Four new sisters, the 'A' liners, were built for the Canadian route. *Andania*, *Antonia*, *Ausonia* and *Aurania* became popular cabin-class ships, both luxurious and relatively cheap to travel on. (JCM)

PLEASURE-CRUISE LIFE IN A LUXURY LINER: THE DELIGHTFUL NEW FORM OF HOLIDAY-MAKING BY OCEAN TOURS AT ALL SEASONS OF

The vogue of ocean touring has increased enormously, and during the coming season this new type of holiday will doubtless prove even more popular. Though the great shipping concerns which run fortnightly trips to the Mediterranean, Atlantic Isles, and Norwegian Fiords do not make a large profit from them, nevertheless they are keeping ships and crews employed and ducating thousands of people to realise what a wonderful life can be enjoyed in a well-appointed British liner; moreover, the money spent goes largely into British pockets. Our illustration shows the Cunard cruising liner "Lancastria" (17,000 tons) gently steaming

in the Straits of Gibraltar and affording passengers their first glimpse of the Rock. To give some idea of the am, magnificent floating hotel, we illustrate the upper deck busy with sports and pastimes, organised by the expert , board known as Cruise Directors. Naturally, all these pastimes would not always be proceeding simultaneously. Besides , there are regular fancy-dress dances on the sports deck when cruising in warm climes; bridge and whist drives, an aquatic sports. For the studious there is the free library, stocked with 2000 books. Lower down in the ship are two or m

43 The inside of a Cunard cruising liner: a cutaway drawing of *Lancastria*. (JCM)

44 Sectional view of *Queen Mary*, at the time the world's largest liner. It helps give an idea of the scale of the public rooms and engines.(JCM)

KITCHENS OF A CRUISING LINER

THE CREW OF A 17,000-TON CRUISING LINER

G PASSENGERS TO SEE THE SIGHTS OF FOREIGN LANDS, WHILE ENJOYING ALL THE AMENITIES ABOARD THEIR OWN "FLOATING HOTEL."

ing-saloons providing good and wholesome food to suit every taste. Unseen by most of the tourists there is another side —the great kitchens, the cooled store-rooms containing vast quantities of food-stuffs, the linen store, and the bakery. The publishes a free newspaper of world news received by wireless, and also the ship's newspaper with all the latest happenings g town. Experts arrange excursions to view the sights ashore. In this way you see the world without having to sleep in or eat food that perhaps may not suit your English digestion, and you have not to be continually packing and unpacking your baggage. In the numerous luxurious public rooms you can have a drink, a game of cards, a laze or a read, and write letters. In the gymnasium you can do your "daily dozen." The ship is large and there is plenty of room for all. It is well found and a good sea-boat. Though the cost of oil-fuel, port dues, and tender charges have to be taken into consideration by the owners, nevertheless the ocean tourist can enjoy all the aforesaid amenities, and see wonderful new sights in foreign lands for little more than one pound per day.—[Drawn Specially for "The Illustrated London News" by G. H. Davis.]

45 The *Queen
Elizabeth* leaves on a
voyage in the early
1960s. (JCM)

46 C.E. Turner's painting of the *Queen Mary*. (JCM)

47 The Captain's Final Voyage under the Blue Ensign.

48 John and Belle, 1970.

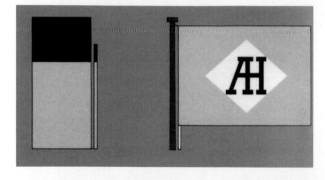

49 The Blue Funnel Line livery.

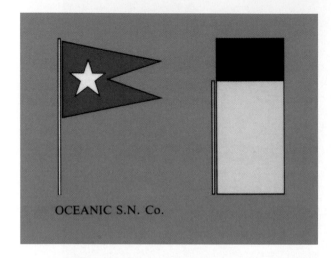

OCEANIC S.N. Co.

50 The White Star Line livery.

CUNARD

CUNARD-WHITE STAR

51 The Cunard Line livery.

Alfred Holt Ltd

The Blue Funnel Line

Funnel	Powder blue with black top.
Hull	Black.
Waterline	Upper strake, flesh pink. Lower plating, dark wine red.
Uppers	Mast vents brown. Funnel clusters, black, others white. Inside of ventilators, blue.
Masts	Chocolate brown or white.

The story goes that when Alfred Holt bought his first steamship she had on board a quantity of bibles, muskets and blue paint. The latter had been used to paint a mourning band around the hull on the death of her previous owner. The remainder of the paint was used by Holt to change the funnel colour, and so the famous Blue Funnel Line was born. Though there are now many companies which use blue as their funnel colour, the shade of the Blue Funnel Line and its successors is unique, the paint being a special mix for the company.

Oceanic Steam Navigation Company

The White Star Line

Funnel	Cream/buff with black top.
Hull	Black, with golden-yellow band.
Waterline	Red.
Uppers	White. Ventilators, white. Inside of cowls, red.
Masts	Funnel colour, with the crow's-nest always white.
Lifeboats	White.

The houseflag of The White Star Line is a 'burgee', as distinct from the more classical oblong flag, or a 'pennant' or a 'swallowtail pennant'.

Cunard Steam Ship Company

The Cunard Line

Funnel	Bright red, containing a tinge of orange. Black top. One to three pin-stripe black bands on the red (these were originally the strengthening hoops of the funnels).

Hull	Black. Cruise ships: white, except for green livery, which was mid-green hull, thin dark green band and pale green uppers.
Waterline	Red, with thin dividing white stripe.
Uppers	White. Ventilators, black or white. Inside of cowls, red.
Masts	Golden-brown.
Lifeboats	White.

One of the accounts for the origins of the particular red/orange colour of the earlier Cunard funnels suggests that it was the colour of the basic anti-rust paint; they simply left it in place and added a black top. Samuel Cunard was reputed to be a Scot with traditional values with regard to the spending of his money.

Cunard – White Star Ltd

The Cunard – White Star Line

Following the merger the vessels retained the funnel colours and liveries of their original owners.

House flags

For many years the new line used the houseflags of both constituents; White Star vessels flying their former houseflag superior, while Cunarders reversed the order. Slowly the White Star influence weakened until in the 1960s the burgee was dispensed with. For a few more years it was worn inferior to the Cunard flag, on one day each year, 20 April, the anniversary of the merger. Even this custom has now lapsed and all trace of White Star has vanished, the company now being known by its Cunard style.

[This information, together with the illustrations of the flags and funnels, has been extracted from the series of books entitled *Merchant Fleets* by Duncan Haws, published by TCL Publications (1996), *A Survey of Mercantile Houseflags & Funnels* by J.L. Loughran, published by Waine Research Publications (1979), and *Brown's Flags and Funnels of Shipping Companies of the World*, by J.L. Loughran, published by Brown, Son & Ferguson (1995).]

52 Captain, *Queen Mary*.

EDITOR'S NOTE

Apart from describing the stories and events during the passing of his life, John has also recalled some of the people who also 'went down to the sea in ships.' Some of them are simply described as significant characters who influenced his perspective of the world:

The first was the mate of one of the first ships he served on as an apprentice, who 'taught me such a lot and trained me to be a real seaman'. There were also the two British managers at the bunkering station of Perrim. 'It was a hell hole to live in and for years on end it must have been almost unbearable.'

Then there were those who, other than the celebrities, were named as being respected and valued acquaintances. There was the Solent Pilot, Captain Jack Holt, who had piloted Queen Mary *in and out of Southampton for many years. 'An excellent Pilot and real fine man who had a fund of good stories.' Also, Mr Hywel Davies, the interviewer and commentator with BBC Wales 'with whom it was a real pleasure to work'.*

However, the one who probably stands out above most of them was the Revd Canon Brady, of the 'Mission to Seamen', in Buenos Aires. John said that 'the Mission is run for the benefit of the seamen, to help look after their morals and welfare in the ports all over the world. They have done, and still do, fine work on our behalf and us seamen are most grateful to them and all those who assist the Missions'.

These days, known as 'The Mission to Seafarers', their work still goes on. Whether it is helping the thirty-five Italian and Romanian crew of a stricken ship in Antwerp, or the twenty-one Nigerian fishermen threatened with shooting and abandoned in port of Aden in the Yemen.

Donations to support this continuing work should be sent to:

> *The Mission to Seafarers*
> *St Michael Paternoster*
> *Royal College Hill*
> *London*
> *EC4R 2RL*

APPENDIX 1

THE FAMILY NAME

CAPT. JOHN TREASURE JONES: THE ORIGINS OF HIS NAME

Many people ask about the origins of the name 'Treasure' Jones. Looking back through the family records there appears to have been a tradition of maintaining a record of the branches in the family tree by giving the sons, the surnames of previous generations as an additional Christian name.

So, the sons of Shrewsbury Treasure Jones (b.1872) were:

Hugh Treasure Jones
John Treasure Jones (b.1905)
Robert Whittow Jones (b.1907)
Henry Devereaux Jones (b.1909)

Since these names were not part of the surname, they were not written with a hyphen.

Treasure

John's father, Shrewsbury Treasure Jones, was the son of Ethelbert (or Jacob) Jones and, it is believed, a Miss Treasure, from Stoke St Michael in Somerset. So this was John's paternal grandmother. The name of Treasure is thought to have links in the County of Somerset.

Whittow

This was the maiden name of John's maternal grandmother, Eleanor Whittow (b.1844), who married Henry Williams in 1866. Robert Whittow Jones, John's brother, married a Gladys Wilmot, and, so continuing the tradition, named their son John Wilmot Jones.

Devereux

This name comes down through John's maternal great-grandfather, John Williams, who married Margaret Devereux. So, there was a James Devereux Williams (b.1872).

APPENDIX 2

SEAMAN'S RECORD BOOK

SUMMARY OF 'CONTINUOUS CERTIFICATE OF DISCHARGE' BOOKS FOR JONES, R21261

Name	Date and place of Engagement	Date and place of Discharge	Rating	Description
–	29/07/1925 HMS Hood	26/01/1926 HMS Ajax	midshipman	6 months' RNR training

Hall Bros of Newcastle

Ambassador 15/02/1926 Barry		18/03/1927 S. Shields	3rd mate	–

3 months' RNR training & Nautical College

Caduseus	09/11/1927 S. Shields	18/02/1928 Barry	2nd mate	–
Caduseus	24/02/1928 Barry	15/06/1928 Cardiff	2nd mate	–
Caduseus	20/06/1928 Cardiff	04/10/1928 Cardiff	2nd mate	–
Caduseus	20/10/1928 Cardiff	21/04/1929 Barry	2nd mate	–

Nautical College & 28 days RNR training

White Star Line

Gallic	26/08/1929 Liverpool	04/09/1929 Tilbury	2nd mate	–
Euripides	09/11/1929 Liverpool	16/01/1930 Brisbane	3rd mate	Australia
Delphic	17/01/1930 Sydney	14/04/1930 Liverpool	2nd mate	Australia

12 months' RNR training, then laid off

Blue Funnel Line

Machaon	01/07/1934 Immingham	22/11/1934 Glasgow	3rd mate	Australia
Machaon	30/01/1935 Birkenhead	06/06/1935 Birkenhead	3rd mate	Far East
Protesilaus	14/09/1935 Birkenhead	25/09/1935 Port Said	3rd mate	Port Said
Rhexenor	02/10/1935 Port Said	16/08/1936 Shanghai	3rd mate	USA & Far East
Rhexenor	16/08/1936 Shanghai	06/10/1936 Singapore	3rd mate	USA & Far East
Theseus	10/10/1936 Singapore	17/11/1936 Birkenhead	3rd mate	–

28 days' RNR training

Cunard White Star Line

Lancastria	25/03/1937 Liverpool	09/04/1937 Liverpool	junior 3rd officer	Cruise
Lancastria	16/04/1937 Liverpool	10/05/1937 London	junior 3rd officer	Montreal

Name	Date and place of Engagement	Date and place of Discharge	Rating	Description
Lancastria	18/05/1937 London	22/06/1937 London	junior 3rd officer	New York
Lancastria	03/07/1937 London	04/10/1937 Liverpool	junior 3rd officer	Cruise
Lancastria	09/10/1937 Liverpool	30/10/1937 Liverpool	junior 3rd officer	Cruise
Lancastria	04/02/1938 Liverpool	01/03/1938 Liverpool	junior 3rd officer	New York
Lancastria	01/04/1938 Liverpool	25/04/1938 Liverpool	junior 3rd officer	New York
Lancastria	05/05/1938 Liverpool	07/06/1938 London	junior 3rd officer	New York
Lancastria	30/06/1938 London	01/10/1938 Liverpool	junior 3rd officer	RA
Aurania	28/10/1938 London	20/11/1938 London	junior 3rd officer	Montreal
Aurania	25/11/1938 London	20/12/1938 London	junior 3rd officer	New York
Britannic	05/01/1939 Liverpool	27/03/1939 Liverpool	senior 3rd officer	West Indies Cruise
Britannic	22/04/1939 Liverpool	05/06/1939 London	senior 3rd officer	New York
Britannic	09/06/1939 London	02/07/1939 London	senior 3rd officer	New York
Britannic	07/07/1939 London	31/07/1939 London	senior 3rd officer	New York
Britannic	04/08/1939 London	27/08/1939 Southampton	senior 3rd officer	New York

RNR Active Service from 09.09.1939 to 01.03.1947

Name	Date and place of Engagement	Date and place of Discharge	Rating	Description
Samaria	17/03/1947 Liverpool	28/04/1947 Liverpool	senior 1st officer	–
Scythia	29/04/1947 Liverpool	23/06/1947 Liverpool	senior 1st officer	–
Scythia	24/06/1947 Liverpool	02/10/1947 Liverpool	senior 1st officer	–
Scythia	03/10/1947 Liverpool	25/11/1947 Liverpool	senior 1st officer	–
Britannic	25/11/1947 Liverpool	31/12/1947 Liverpool	senior 1st officer	–
Georgic	05/03/1948 Southampton	17/04/1948 Southampton	senior 1st officer	–
Queen Elizabeth	20/04/1948 Southampton	22/06/1948 Southampton	senior 1st officer	New York
Queen Elizabeth	07/07/1948 Southampton	14/09/1948 Southampton	chief officer	New York
Queen Elizabeth	29/09/1948 Southampton	13/11/1948 Southampton	chief officer	New York
Queen Elizabeth	13/12/1948 Southampton	01/04/1949 Southampton	chief officer	–
Queen Elizabeth	19/04/1949 Southampton	21/06/1949 Southampton	chief officer	–
Queen Elizabeth	08/07/1949 Southampton	26/09/1949 Southampton	chief officer	–
Queen Elizabeth	12/10/1949 Southampton	29/11/1949 Southampton	chief officer	–
Queen Elizabeth	16/12/1949 Southampton	04/04/1950 Southampton	chief officer	New York
Queen Elizabeth	19/04/1950 Southampton	22/05/1950 Southampton	chief officer	New York
Samaria	03/06/1950 London	28/07/1950 London	chief officer	–
Samaria	29/07/1950 London	23/11/1950 Liverpool	chief officer	–
Ascania	24/11/1950 Liverpool	28/12/1950 Liverpool	chief officer	–
Ascania	22/01/1951 Liverpool	13/03/1951 London	chief officer	–

RN War College at Greenwich 28.03.1951 to 03.08.1951

Name	Date and place of Engagement	Date and place of Discharge	Rating	Description
Samaria	07/08/1951 Southampton	20/12/1951 Southampton	chief officer	Quebec
Queen Elizabeth	12/03/1952 Southampton	13/05/1952 Southampton	chief officer	New York
Queen Elizabeth	27/05/1952 Southampton	24/07/1952 Southampton	chief officer	New York
Queen Elizabeth	12/08/1952 Southampton	25/08/1952 Southampton	chief officer	New York
Queen Elizabeth	09/09/1952 Southampton	04/11/1952 Southampton	chief officer	New York
Queen Elizabeth	19/11/1952 Southampton	02/02/1953 Southampton	chief officer	New York
Queen Elizabeth	03/02/1953 Southampton	12/03/1953 Southampton	chief officer	New York
Queen Elizabeth	30/03/1953 Southampton	12/05/1953 Southampton	staff captain	New York
Mauretania	23/05/1953 Southampton	27/06/1953 Southampton	staff captain	New York
Vandalia	???	???	master	–
Queen Elizabeth	09/09/1953 Southampton	22/09/1953 Southampton	staff captain	New York
Mauretania	28/09/1953 Southampton	07/10/1953 Southampton	staff captain	New York
Queen Mary	28/10/1953 Southampton	03/12/1953 Southampton	chief officer	New York
Queen Elizabeth	08/12/1953 Southampton	25/01/1954 Southampton	staff captain	New York
Queen Mary	18/02/1954 Southampton	21/04/1954 Southampton	staff captain	–
Queen Mary	05/05/1954 Southampton	30/06/1954 Southampton	staff captain	–
Queen Mary	20/07/1954 Southampton	31/08/1954 Southampton	staff captain	–
Caronia	15/09/1954 Southampton	04/08/1955 Southampton	staff captain	World Cruise
Queen Elizabeth	06/09/1955 Southampton	19/10/1955 Southampton	staff captain	–
Queen Mary	23/11/1955 Southampton	30/01/1956 Southampton	staff captain	New York
Queen Mary	20/03/1956 Southampton	02/05/1956 Southampton	staff captain	New York
Queen Mary	16/05/1956 Southampton	12/07/1956 Southampton	staff captain	New York
Mauretania	09/08/1956 Southampton	17/09/1956 Southampton	staff captain	New York

RN Tactical School at Woolwich 19.09.1956 to 30.11.1956

Name	Date and place of Engagement	Date and place of Discharge	Rating	Description
Queen Mary	06/12/1956 Southampton	15/05/1957 Southampton	staff captain	–
Media	24/05/1957 Liverpool	30/11/1957 Liverpool	master	–
Media	06/12/1957 Liverpool	31/05/1958 Liverpool	master	–
Media	01/06/1958 Liverpool	20/02/1959 Liverpool	master	–
Sylvania	20/02/1959 Liverpool	14/03/1959 Liverpool	master	–
Media	28/03/1959 Liverpool	16/05/1959 Liverpool	master	–
Media	17/05/1959 Liverpool	11/07/1959 Liverpool	master	–
Saxonia	26/08/1959 Southampton	14/12/1959 Southampton	master	–
Saxonia	15/12/1959 Southampton	25/03/1960 Southampton	master	–
Saxonia	11/06/1960 Southampton	27/07/1960 Southampton	master	–
Saxonia	16/08/1960 Southampton	21/12/1960 Southampton	master	–
Saxonia	22/12/1960 Southampton	15/02/1961 Southampton	master	–
Saxonia	15/03/1961 Southampton	09/06/1961 Southampton	master	–
Saxonia	05/07/1961 Southampton	13/10/1961 Southampton	master	–

Name	Date and place of Engagement	Date and place of Discharge	Rating	Description
Saxonia	23/12/1961 Liverpool	06/04/1962 Southampton	master	–
Saxonia	23/05/1962 Southampton	29/06/1962 Southampton	master	–
Saxonia	30/06/1962 Southampton	20/07/1962 Southampton	master	–
Saxonia	14/08/1962 Southampton	29/09/1962 Southampton	master	–
Carinthia	24/10/1962 Liverpool	12/11/1962 Southampton	master	–
Mauretania	04/12/1962 Southampton	07/04/1963 Naples	master	–
Mauretania	02/05/1963 Naples	05/08/1963 Naples	master	–
Mauretania	21/09/1963 Naples	20/02/1964 Southampton	master	–
Mauretania	06/03/1964 Southampton	01/06/1964 Southampton	master	–
Mauretania	23/06/1964 Southampton	08/10/1964 Southampton	master	–
Mauretania	26/10/1964 Southampton	14/01/1965 Southampton	master	–
Mauretania	24/02/1965 Southampton	30/04/1965 Southampton	master	–
Mauretania	15/05/1965 Southampton	23/06/1965 Southampton	master	–
Queen Elizabeth	07/07/1965 Southampton	20/07/1965 Southampton	master	–
Queen Mary	08/09/1965 Southampton	14/09/1965 New York	master	–
Mauretania	15/09/1965 New York	23/11/1965 Inverkeithing	master	–
Queen Mary	30/12/1965 Southampton	30/03/1966 Southampton	master	–
Queen Mary	27/04/1966 Southampton	03/08/1966 Southampton	master	–
Queen Mary	17/08/1966 Southampton	28/09/1966 Southampton	master	–
Queen Mary	13/10/1966 Southampton	21/11/1966 Southampton	master	–
Queen Mary	07/12/1966 Southampton	07/03/1967 Southampton	master	–
Queen Mary	22/03/1967 Southampton	16/04/1967 Southampton	master	–
Queen Mary	15/05/1967 Southampton	19/07/1967 Southampton	master	–
Queen Mary	16/08/1967 Southampton	11/12/1967 Long Beach	master	–

Name	Association From	Association To	Total Years Service	Rating	Months
Caronia	15/09/1954	04/08/1955	0.88	staff captain	World Cruise
Media	24/05/1957	11/07/1959	2.01	master	–
Mauretania	23/05/1953	23/11/1965	2.47	staff captain	2.73
Mauretania	–	–	–	master	26.89
Saxonia	26/08/1959	29/09/1962	2.28	master	–
Queen Elizabeth	20/04/1948	20/07/1965	2.96	chief officer	30.25
Queen Elizabeth	–	–	–	staff captain	4.83
Queen Elizabeth	–	–	–	master	One round trip
Queen Mary	28/10/1953	11/12/1967	3.00	chief officer	Three round trips
Queen Mary	–	–	–	staff captain	16.04
Queen Mary	–	–	–	master	18.81

THE MERCHANT SHIPS – SUMMARY

THE MERCHANT SHIPS IN THE LIFE OF CAPTAIN JOHN TREASURE JONES

Name	Built	GRT	No. of Passengers	No. of Crew
J.C. Gould Steamship Co. of Cardiff – (1921 to 1925)				
Grelgrant	1906	4,785 tons	–	–
Grelhead	1915	4,274 tons	–	–
Hall Bros of Newcastle – (1926 to 1929)				
Ambassador	1925	4,450 tons	–	–
Caduceus	1927	4,364 tons	–	–
The White Star Line – (1929 to 1931)				
Euripides[1]	1914	14,974 tons	–	–
Delphic	1918	8,006 tons	–	–
Alfred Holt Ltd, The Blue Funnel Line – (1934 to 1936)				
Machaon 2	1920	7,806 tons	–	–
Rhexenor	1922	7,957 tons	–	–
The Cunard–White Star Line – (1937 to 1968)				
Lancastria	1922	16,243 tons	1,891	310
Britannic[2]	1930	26,943 tons	1,553	500
Samaria	1921	19,597 tons	2,200	434
Scythia	1921	19,730 tons	2,200	434
Ascania	1925	14,013 tons	1,448	270
Caronia	1949	34,274 tons	930	600
Vandalia[3]	**1943**	**7,273 tons**	**cargo**	–
Media	**1947**	**13,345 tons**	**250**	**184**
Sylvania	**1957**	**22,017 tons**	**896**	**460**
Saxonia	**1954**	**22,592 tons**	**925**	**457**
Carinthia 3	**1956**	**21,947 tons**	**856**	**461**
Mauretania 2	**1939**	**35,793 tons**	**1,127**	**560**
Queen Elizabeth	**1940**	**83,673 tons**	**2,283**	**1,296**
Queen Mary	**1936**	**81,235 tons**	**1,995**	**1,285**

NB: those ships in **bold** identify ships served 'in command'.
The full list of ships appears in Appendix 2 taken from his Seaman's Record Book

THE CUNARD WHITE STAR LINERS – DETAILS

THE CUNARD WHITE STAR LINERS IN THE LIFE
OF CAPTAIN JOHN TREASURE JONES

Name	Built	GRT	Total Passengers	First Class	Second 'cabin' Class	Third 'tourist' Class	Crew	Other Details
Lancastria	1922	16,243 tons	1,891	265	370	1,256	310	sunk June 1940, St Nazaire
Britannic	1930	26,943 tons	1,553	–	504	1,049	500	–
Britannic refit	1947	27,666 tons	993	429	–	564		scrapped Dec. 1960
Samaria	1921	19,597 tons	2,200	350	350	1,500	434	–
Samaria refit	1949	–	900	250	–	650	–	scrapped January 1956
Scythia	1921	19,730 tons	2,200	350	350	1,500	434	–
Scythia refit	1949	19,930 tons	878	248	–	630	–	scrapped Jan. 1958
Ascania	1925	14,013 tons	1,448	–	520	928	270	–
Ascania refit	1949	–	700	200	–	500	–	scrapped Dec. 1956
Caronia	1949	34,274 tons	930	580	–	350	600	scrapped April 1974
Media	**1947**	**13,345 tons**	**250**	**250**	**–**	**–**	**184**	**sold 1961 (scrapped 1989)**
Sylvania	**1957**	**22,017 tons**	**896**	**172**	**–**	**724**	**460**	**sold 1968**
Saxonia	**1954**	**22,592 tons**	**925**	**125**	**–**	**800**	**457**	**sold 1973**
Carinthia 3	**1956**	**21,947 tons**	**856**	**174**	**–**	**682**	**461**	**sold 1968**
Mauretania 2	**1939**	**35,739 tons**	**1,169**	**475**	**390**	**304**	**593**	**–**

Name	Built	GRT	Total Passengers	First Class	Second 'cabin' Class	Third 'tourist' Class	Crew	Other Details
Mauretania 2 **refit**	1962	–	1,127	406	364	357	560	scrapped Nov 1965
Queen Elizabeth	1940	83,673 tons	2,283	823	662	798	1,296	burnt out Jan 1972
Queen Mary	1936	81,235 tons	1,995	711	707	577	1,285	sold Dec 1967

NB: those ships in **bold** identify ships served 'in command'.

Sources:

Vard, Kenneth, *Liners in Art* (Halsgrove: 2001)

Rentell, Philip, *Historic Cunard Liners* (Atlantic Transport Publishers: 1986)

Card, Stephen J., *Cunarder: Maritime Paintings* (Carmania Press: 2003)

APPENDIX 5

THE FAMOUS PEOPLE

THE FAMOUS PEOPLE I HAVE MET OVER THE YEARS

King George VI, Queen Elizabeth and Princess Margaret in June 1948, when they visited RMS *Queen Elizabeth* to view the magnificent portrait of Queen Elizabeth which was hung in the Main Lounge. I was senior first officer of the ship and duty officer that day, and was presented to them. In 1964, whilst captain of RMS *Mauretania*, I hosted Queen Elizabeth, then Queen Mother, to lunch aboard when she opened the Texaco Oil Refinery at Milford Haven. Lastly, on 3 May 1986, I was again presented to her on *QE2* at an event to celebrate the 50th Anniversary of the *Queen Mary*;
The Duke and Duchess of Windsor;
Sir Winston Churchill and family;
Anthony Eden, Lord Avon, who was Prime Minister during the Suez Crisis;
Lord Louis Mountbatten;
President Eisenhower when he was a general;
Field Marshal Montgomery;
Estée and Joe Lauder of the Cosmetics Company;
Alfred Bloomingdale of Diners Club;
Harry Randolph of Wilkinson Sword;
Yehudi Menuhin, Sir Alec Guinness, Deborah Kerr, Joan Crawford, Anna Neagle, Gracie Fields, Arthur Hitchcock, Michael Wilding, Margaret Rutherford, Rita Hayworth, Julie Andrews, Robert Stack, Greer Garson, Helen O'Connell, Johnny Mathis, Tessa O'Shea, Liberace, Beatrice Lillie.

During and after the final cruise of *Queen Mary*:
Sir John Russell, British Ambassador to Brazil
The President of Peru
Ronald Reagan, Governor of California

APPENDIX 6

APPOINTMENTS AND SALARIES

1921, per the terms of the Apprentice's Indenture, total salary of £40 over four years:

First year	£6 p.a.
Second year	£8
Third year	£11
Fourth year	£15

Plus £12 in the last year in lieu of 'Washing':

> The master agrees to provide the Apprentice with sufficient Meat, Drink, Lodging, &, except when in the United Kingdom, with ('Washing' is crossed out) Medicine, and Medical and Surgical Assistance.

1946	captain RNR	£1,825 p.a.
1947	first officer, *Scythia*	£576
01/05/1955	staff captain, *Coronia*	£1,500
08/09/1955	staff captain, *Queen Elizabeth*	£1,835
01/01/1957	staff captain, *Queen Mary*	£2,055
25/05/1957	captain, *Media*	£2,055
01/07/1957	captain, *Media*	£2,190
01/08/1958	captain, *Media*	reduction to £2,090 (from introduction of 'Top Hat' pension scheme)
01/11/1958	captain, *Media*	£2,200
20/02/1959	captain, *Sylvania*	£2,625
26/08/1959	captain, *Saxonia*	–
04/12/1962	captain, *Mauretania*	–
02/02/1966	captain, *Queen Mary*	–
11/12/1967	–	less than £4,000

NOTES:

1. Sometimes, wages paid while on leave were lower than when serving at sea.
2. By comparison, the editor, recently qualified as a Chartered Accountant, joined an electronics company, aged 22 in 1967 to earn £1,000 per year. They didn't get much then and the job is still poorly paid compared to other jobs with similar responsibilities.

RNR RECORDS – RANKS & SERVICE

Captain John Treasure Jones, RD, RNR, date of birth: 18 August 1905.

RANKS HELD:

Rank	Age	From	To
Probationary midshipman	18	11 Sep. 1923	17 Mar. 1926
midshipman	20	18 Mar. 1926	17 Aug. 1926
acting sub lieutenant	21	18 Aug. 1926	08 Jan. 1928
sub lieutenant	22	09 Jan. 1928	17 Aug. 1929
lieutenant	24	18 Aug. 1929	17 Aug. 1937
lieutenant-commander	32	18 Aug. 1937	29 Jun. 1943
commander	37	30 Jun. 1943	30 Dec. 1949
captain	44	31 Dec. 1949	18 Aug. 1960

SHIPS:

Name	Type of Ship	Date of Engagement	Date of Discharge
HMS *Hood*	Battle-Cruiser	29 Jul. 1925	28 Nov 1925
HMS *Velox*	Destroyer	29 Nov. 1925	07 Jan. 1926
HMS *Ajax*	Battleship	08 Jan. 1926	26 Jan. 1926
HMS *Adventure*	Minelayer	16 May 1927	03 Jul. 1927
HMS *Vivien*	Destroyer	02 Jul. 1929	30 Jul. 1929
HMS *Glorious*	Cruiser/ Aircraft Carrier	03 Jan. 1931	03 Jul. 1931
HMS *Viscount*	Destroyer	04 Jul. 1931	31 Oct. 1931
HMS *Wild Swan*	Destroyer	25 Nov. 1936	22 Dec. 1936
AMC *Laurentic*	AMC	09 Sept. 1939	unknown
HMS *Sunflower*	Corvette	18 Dec. 1940	19 Feb. 1943
HMS *Wellington*	Sloop	04 Mar. 1943	18 Jun. 1943
HMS *Baynton*	Frigate	19 Jun. 1943	29 Aug. 1943
HMS *Dart*	Frigate	30 Aug. 1943	31 May 1945

DECORATIONS AND MEDALS:

1939-45 Star
Atlantic Star
Africa Star, with Bar for North Africa 1942-43
1939-45 War Medal, with oak leaf for mention in Despatches
Coronation Medal
Reserve Decoration, with Bar (for the equivalent of 44½ service years)

SHIPS:

Name	Type of Ship	Built	Tons	Class	Other Details
HMS *Hood*	Battle–Cruiser	1918	41,200	–	sunk May 1941 by *Bismarck*
HMS *Velox*	Destroyer	1917	1,300	V/W Class	sold 1947
HMS *Ajax*	Battleship	1912	23,000	–	sold 1926
HMS *Adventure*	Minelayer	1924	6,740	–	sold 1947
HMS *Vivien*	Destroyer	1918	1,300	V/W Class	sold 1947
HMS *Glorious*	Cruiser	1916	18,600	1st Class Cruiser	sunk June 1940 at Narvik
	Aircraft Carrier	1930	converted		
HMS *Viscount*	Destroyer	1917	1,300	V/W Class	sold 1945
HMS *Wild Swan*	Destroyer	1919	1,300	Modified W Class	sunk June 1942
AMC *Laurentic*	Armed Merchant Cruiser	1927	18,724	–	sunk November 1940
HMS *Sunflower*	Corvette – K41	1940	1,100	Flower Class	–
HMS *Wellington*	Sloop – U65	1934	990	–	sold 1947
HMS *Baynton*	Frigate – K310	1942	1,250	Captain Class	lease-lend to 1945
HMS *Dart*	Frigate – K21	1942	1,375	River Class	–

Laurentic: Built for White Star Line. Last major Atlantic liner with coal fired, triple expansion engines. On 18 August 1935 she was involved in a serious collision with the Blue Star Liner Napier Star and was laid up. Apart from a trooping voyage to Palestine in 1936, she remained idle until being commissioned as an Armed Merchant Cruiser in 1939

SHORE ESTABLISHMENTS:

Ship	Location	From	To
HMS *Vivid*	Plymouth (Gunnery)	04 Apr. 1927	15 May 1927
HMS *Victory*	Portsmouth (Signals)	01 Nov. 1930	21 Nov. 1930
HMS *Vernon*	Torpedo School	22 Nov. 1930	05 Dec. 1930
HMS *Vivid*	Plymouth (Gunnery)	06 Dec. 1930	02 Jan. 1931
HMS *Defiance*	Shore Base (Torpedo)	10 Mar. 1934	23 Mar. 1934
HMS *Drake*	Shore Base (Gunnery)	24 Mar. 1934	06 Apr. 1934
HMS *Pembroke*	Accounting Base	unknown	04 Dec. 1940
HMS *Nimrod*	Shore Base	05 Dec. 1940	17 Dec. 1940
HMS *Pembroke*	Accounting Base	20 Feb. 1943	03 Mar. 1943
HMS *Drake*	Shore Base	01 Jun. 1945	23 Jun. 1945
HMS *Lucifer*	Swansea Shore Base	24 Jan. 1945	24 Jul. 1945
HMS *Eaglet*	Liverpool Shore Base	25 Jul. 1945	07 Sep. 1945
HMS *Hathi*	Kandy, Ceylon SO Eastern Fleet	08 Sep. 1945	27 Sep. 1945
HMS *Sultan*	Singapore Accounting	28 Sep. 1945	01 Mar. 1947
HMS *President*	London, Reserve Drill Ship	–	–
HMS *President*	1 day training: Operation Trident	13 Apr 1949	13 Apr 1949
RN War College Greenwich Senior Officers War Course		28 Mar 1951	03 Aug 1951
RN Tactical School Woolwich Senior Officers War Tactical Course		17 Sep 1956	30 Nov 1956

Prior to 1959, the Naval Discipline Act only applied to those officers and men who were borne on the books of one of His/Her Majesty's Ships of War (HMS). Thus all personnel were allocated to a nominal ship or 'stone-frigate' when not actually serving in a proper seagoing warship.

APPENDIX 8

HMS SUNFLOWER

HMS *Sunflower* (K41) was launched on 19 August 1940. The Flower Class Corvettes were designed to escort and defend merchant shipping from U-boat attacks. They were capable of approximately 16 knots and, at that speed the range was 2,360 nautical miles. At 10 knots the range went up to 5,000 nautical miles. They were definitely not designed for comfort. It was said of these Corvettes that they could stay at sea in all weathers.

In the Sunflower's case the armament consisted of a 4 inch gun, manufactured in 1914, and a single barrelled pom-pom gun mounted on a raised platform mid-ship. The starboard and port side well-decks each had a depth-charge thrower. It was a difficult process for three men, with the deck heaving up and down, to load a depth-charge and its stork into the fixed K-Gun thrower which was bolted to the deck. When this was complete, a charge was placed in the base of the K-Gun and Depth Pistol was set. The rating in charge would pull the firing toggle and away went the depth-charge and stork, high in the air and well away from the ship's side.

On the stern were two chutes with depth-charges, all ready primed and only requiring a 'depth' to be set before being released off the stern. There were two further storage racks of depth-charges, all primed and ready to replace those that had been dropped. We carried approximately sixty-five depth-charges.

The ships compliment was approximately sixty-five officer and ratings. In 1942 the ship's company was made up of British, Newfoundland (it was not part of Canada at this time) and Canadian ratings, all volunteers.

John Dixon recalls that in early December 1942:

> We departed Londonderry to join the westbound convoy of forty-three merchant ships (codename ON153) to be part of the escort which consisted of four corvettes:
>
> > *Sunflower*, *Pink*, *Alisma* and *Loosestrife* (possibly HMS *Kingcup*)
>
> The two destroyers were:
>
> > *Firedrake* (H79) and *Ripley* (G79), which was originally USS *Shubrick*.
>
> The Wolf Pack 'Raufbold' sighted our convoy on 15 December It consisted of thirteen U-boats:
>
> > U135, U203, U211, U365, U409, U410, U600, U609, U610, U621, U623 and U664
>
> As soon as darkness fell, the U-boats began their attack. The U365 sinks a tanker, then U610 sinks another tanker, a freighter falls victim to U621.
>
> Late in the evening of 16 December, we were at the position 51.00'north by 25.00'west. Action Stations had been sounded; my station was cordite supply to the 4-inch gun. I was standing on the gun platform with the cordite container on my left shoulder, ready to supply a reduced charge of cordite to the breach loader.
>
> The mountainous waves were coming over the bows and drenching the gun's crew. It was freezing cold, a gale force wind was blowing and the only clothing I had on was a pair of socks, sandshoes, underwear and a pair of overalls with my lifejacket strapped around my chest.

Stan Clark was part of the gun crew and recalls that:

> Our radio operator had reported to our captain that he couldn't contact the *Firedrake*, we could see star shells exploding in the sky about five miles or so south of the convoy, but we couldn't leave

Crew-member's sketch of HMS *Sunflower*.

our station which was on the west of the convoy. After several hours trying to contact Firedrake, the captain decided to see what was happening south of the convoy, so we were called to Action Stations and steamed at full speed to where the action was. As we got closer the captain thought he could see a U-boat on the surface. So we were ordered to load with 'HE' (high explosive), then waited for the order to fire. As we got closer he could see that it was not a U-boat, but, in fact, the remains of the *Firedrake* which had been cut in two with only the stern still afloat. We were ordered to unload the 'HE' and reload with Star Shell and fire above the wreck. The first round failed to spark up, so we fired another which did light up so that we all could see the smashed wreck of which was the *Firedrake*.

John Dixon's account continues:

Stand Down from Action Stations was sounded. The captain of the gun told me to go and get some warm clothing on then, with other ratings, go down into the starboard well-deck to put the scrambling net over the ship's side. This net was there for the very reason it was being used this very night. There was another net situated on the port side. I could just make out that some of the survivors were on the stern section of the *Firedrake*, other survivors were hanging on to a floating cork net about 30 yards off our starboard beam. The corvette was going up and down like a yo-yo. It was then that one of our party, a Newfoundland rating by the name of Furey, with a heaving line tied round his chest, lowered himself down the scrambling net into the freezing cold sea. He set off to swim towards the floating cork net. When he finally arrived he entwined his arms in the netting and so became a human link in the towing line. We then pulled the corked net alongside the *Sunflower*. Able-seaman Furey remained in the sea to assist the men up and onto the heaving deck. He swam out to individual men in the water, grabbed hold of them while the two on the other end of the rope pulled him back to the ship. He managed to bring back twenty-eight of them, but, sadly the last man he brought to the rail of the *Sunflower* slipped from his arms as he was too exhausted to hold him any longer. He was never to receive a medal for his bravery for this action (although he did receive a mention in Dispatches, published in the *London Gazette* of 23 March 1943, three months before his captain).

Whilst this very brave action was taking place, the starboard bridge communication signal lamp was being used intermittently to spot other survivors. It was being used in this manner in fear of becoming a second target for a U-boat. In the beam of the light, a rubber dinghy was momentarily illuminated with two men inboard. One of them was stretched out, in the bottom not moving, the other man had a small paddle which he was using in an attempt to make his way towards our ship's side. The moment the light had flashed on him I heard him call out to us to help the men in the water first, before rescuing them both. They were probably stokers from the *Firedrake's* boiler room as they only had vests and trouser overalls on. The hands of the man who was paddling were blackened and appeared to be badly burned, but he seemed to be void of pain.

After we had all the survivors safely on board, the *Sunflower* moved off to continue her escort duties. Two of the merchant ships were unable to maintain the speed of the convoy owing to the atrocious weather. They fell further and further behind and both were sunk by U621; the *Otina* (UK) on 20th and the *Oropos* (Greek) on 21 December.

After approximately three weeks at sea I found serving aboard a Corvette very wearing, with the extreme cold, never being in a dry environment and the constant pressure of the U-boats. There was not much chance of survival if we were torpedoed; with so few compartments the ship would sink in seconds. Living and sleeping conditions were very cramped in the forecastle for the seamen, but not too bad for the officers and petty officers. Once the perishable food was consumed after about four days from leaving port it was tinned corned beef for the three meals a day. I must say at this point that I did like, and still do, 'Corned Dog' as we used to refer to it.

This Wolf Pack 'Raufbold', in its short life, was responsible for the sinking of seventy ships. The U-boat that torpedoed the *Firedrake*, U211, under the commander Lieutenant Commander Hause, was herself sunk 430 miles SW of Cape Finisterre on 19 November 1943 by a Wellington of Coastal Command fitted with a Leigh Light; there was possibly only one survivor, Karl-Heinz Schmidt-Rosemann.

Extracted from the website www.carlsen.karoo.net.

APPENDIX 9

HMS FIREDRAKE

On the night of 16 December 1942, HMS *Firedrake*, an 'F' class Destroyer, was the escort leader to convoy ON153, with forty-three ships bound for Canada. They sailed into a force 12 storm, the worst the Atlantic had seen for a very long time. At about 17.00 hrs, the ASDIC operator picked up a contact. HMS *Firedrake* tracked the contact to about five miles south of the convoy, when at 20.10 hrs she was hit by a torpedo fired by U-boat U211. The ship broke in two. The bow section sank immediately, with the stern just managing to stay afloat.

Lieutenant D.J. Dampier RN had a tally up and found there were thirty-five still on board. He quickly got the men to work shoring up the bulkheads of No. 3 boiler room, and making safe and jettisoning the depth charges and torpedoes. The gun crew were ordered to fire star shells to attract the attention of the other escorts, because all the radio and signalling equipment had gone with the bow part of the ship.

At about 22.00 hrs, one of the other escorts – HMS *Sunflower*, a Flower class Corvette, was attracted by the star shells so she made towards them, firing star shells herself. The skipper first thought that the stern section of *Firedrake* was a U-boat and was about to fire HE at it, but then suddenly realised what it was. He tried to get his ship as close as possible to HMS *Firedrake* in order to get the survivors off, but the weather was so bad and the sea too rough. There were 60ft waves breaking over the two ships, which were bobbing about like corks, so he decided to stand by and hope the weather would get better. At about 00.40 hrs on 17 December, the weather worsened and the bulkheads started to give way under the tremendous battering. The stern of HMS *Firedrake* started to sink, so the men had no option but to take to the water, and at 00.45hr the stern sank. The *Sunflower* moved in quickly to pick up the men in the water, a Newfoundland rating; G.J. Furey, had a rope tied around his waist and was lowered down the side of *Sunflower*. He would swim out to a man and grab hold of him, and then his mates onboard would heave them back to the ship and get him onboard. He and his mates managed to get twenty-seven onboard, but one died later. There were 168 of the *Firedrake*'s crew lost and three others that had been picked up earlier that had survived an earlier sinking that night.

Extracted from the website www.hmsfiredrake.co.uk

APPENDIX 10

ANOTHER PERSPECTIVE

In Chapter 5, John describes moving back from the liners to be the master of the freighter *Vandalia*:

> Life aboard the Liners, even for the officer and men, was undoubtedly very good. In the post-war years it would have been 'the lap of luxury' compared with the life on shore, where, in the UK, rationing continued for many years. Even so, sometimes this style of life palled for someone who had grown up on a farm, and whose life up to and including the war years had been anything but luxurious.

Just recently we came into contact with Alan Norman who, in his early days at sea, had worked closely with John. He has some interesting memories and observations about that time. This is his story:

> I was born in my grandmother's house in Christchurch but moved to Highcliffe in the winter of 1946. Highcliffe was very parochial in those days and the village lads usually ended up as customs officers or in local government, both of which had no appeal for me. My ambition was to be a navigator on the airlines or with the Cunard Line. My dad had two very close pals, one a flight engineer with BOAC and the other a steward with Cunard Line. They met regularly in the Highcliffe Men's Club where many stories unfolded and I became privy to their fascinating world of travel and exotic destinations. However, it wasn't until I met my careers officer at school that I discovered that I was colour blind on red and green. This was a bombshell for me and I realised immediately that becoming a navigator of either sort would not be possible. I got over the shock eventually but still had my sights set on travelling. Now that I couldn't join an airline, I embarked on my next journey and that was to join the Cunard Line.
>
> Against the reluctance of my dad, I joined the Merchant Navy in 1962, but first had to attend the Training Ship *Vindicatrix*, the National Sea Training College, in order to gain disciplines in seamanship and catering. After my stint on TS *Vindicatrix*, I was ready to join my first ship, which was the RMS *Transvaal Castle*, sailing in December 1962 from Southampton to South Africa. She was part of the Union Castle Line, a new ship and very well appointed, just two to a cabin. My job was that of a 'boy rating' attached to the Purser's Office, delivering telegrams and messages. After two trips to the Cape, the opportunity came whereby I had the chance to join the Cunard Liner RMS *Mauretania*, which was about to commence a new service between Italy and New York. So I was flown out to Naples aboard a Comet belonging to BOAC Cunard and my dream became reality.
>
> On board the *Mauretania* I was at first attached to the Writer's Office, once again delivering messages and typing out cocktail invitations for the captain. After a month I was then offered the opportunity to work with the captain's 'tiger', waiting at the Captain's Table, as a commis waiter.[1] The position of the captain's tiger could be compared to that of an officer's Batman in the armed forces.
>
> I did this for almost two years and enjoyed every moment working with the tiger, Gordon Whelan,[2] who taught me so much about the catering side of the industry. Our role was to serve at the Captain's Table for all meals, as well as to serve cocktails and canapés in the captain's cabin when he held functions for the guests on his table. Gordon would also be responsible for the cleaning of the cabin and making the captain's bed. My main function was to prepare the table,

depending on the meal and the weather, cleaning the table silver each morning, ensuring the table linen was clean and folded correctly, as well as assisting Gordon serve at the table. At breakfast times I usually served the table alone, as Gordon would be carrying out his other duties in the captain's cabin.

The captain was very much a 'man of habit' regarding his food. Some of his favourite dishes, and remember I am going back forty-four years, were:

As an appetiser, he regularly had Grapefruit Jamaica.
For lunch, a favourite was Cream of Tripe, with a splash of vinaigrette dressing.
At least once a week, for dinner, he always enjoyed Duck with Wild Rice and Asparagus, served with a relish called Bar-le-Duc.
He was also very partial to Caviar Blinis, Lobster Thermidor and Lobster Newberg.
Several times a week he would also have a custard pudding for dessert with lunch.
As a dessert after dinner, he always enjoyed Baked Alaska.

I was not aware of the alcohol policy in my early days, but today there is a very strict code concerning the alcohol policy onboard all ships. However officers did, and still do, enjoy a great social life onboard, hosting tables and attending cocktail parties. I never served the captain with other than his favourite tipple, freshly squeezed orange juice. Occasionally one of his guests would challenge him that it contained gin or vodka, but it was his custom not to drink alcohol whilst at sea.

I first met Captain Treasure Jones in April of 1963, when I joined the ship in Naples. In his function, he was an extremely busy person, but always completed his inspections of the ship each week, barring any adverse weather conditions. These inspections included all areas of the ship, with all the Heads of Departments. There was generally an inspection on Sunday mornings, after he had led the church service. He would return to his cabin and then give notice which department he would visit; in the time it took for him to enjoy a leisurely cup of coffee, they had the time to ensure that everything was ship-shape. He was the archetypal Cunard Ship's master. In the two years that I knew him he was always the consummate professional and exuded confidence. If he had a reputation, it was that of a strict but fair man and a very capable seaman, someone you could trust to make the right decision with regards to the safety of the ship, passengers and crew.

I remember well, that on 23 November 1963 we were berthed in New York. The captain was just settling down to lunch with the President of the Cunard American operations. As usual we had a transistor radio on in the pantry, when it was announced that President Kennedy had been assassinated. I was dispatched by Gordon Whelan to tell the captain, and he and his guest immediately left the table to go in search of further news.

In December 1964 I was transferred to the *Queen Elizabeth*. Over the years I served on all the Cunard Liners, sadly, with the exception of the *Queen Mary*. I finally retired from the sea in 2005, having reached the rank of hotel manager/chief purser; my last ship was the *QE2*.

The memories of what John's favourite dishes were at sea, mirrors the simple type of food he enjoyed when he was at home.

A good, plainly cooked, Steak
Roasted leg of Welsh Lamb
Pigs' Trotters
Tripe and Onions
Cabbage, Parsnip and Swede

Even though he made it a rule not to drink whilst at sea, on shore he enjoyed a pint of beer, particularly after a round of golf or a game of cricket. In the evenings, as a 'nightcap', he and Belle would often have a whiskey. His favourite brands were *Famous Grouse* and *Jim Beam*. Occasionally this would stretch to 'the other wing', as he invariably described a second glass.

APPENDIX 11

THE BLUE ENSIGN

The Blue Ensign originally denoted the rear admiral's squadron when the Royal Navy was divided into three squadrons in 1617. This system using the familiar red, white and blue ensigns to denote each one was abolished in 1864. The Royal Navy retained the White, and the Red Ensign was given to the merchant navy. Since 1861 however, Royal Naval Reserve captains are entitled to fly the Blue Ensign when in command of their merchant ships. There was an additional stipulation that at least seven other officers and men on the crew were also Royal Naval Reservists.

The first captains of both the *Queen Mary* and the *Mauretania 2* were RNR and the various paintings by Charles Pears, Stephen Card and Harley Crossley of these liners at the time of their maiden voyages correctly depict them flying the Blue Ensign. Captain John Treasure Jones was the last master of each these two great liners. After having had the command of the *Mauretania 2* for several years, he took her for her final voyage to the scrap-yard at Inverkeithing, Scotland in November 1965. He then took command of the *Queen Mary* for her final two years at sea, which ended when she arrived in Long Beach in December 1967.

As distinct from the Red Ensign, the Blue tended to be the personal property of the captain. John kept his in a particular attaché case. The story is told that when coming aboard he would call for the Yeoman of Signals and give him the express command that, when the ensign was not flying, it was to be returned each time to its special case.

Capt. John Treasure Jones' first command of a Cunard passenger ship was the *Media*. In the painting by Stephen Card, illustrated in *Liners in Art* by Kenneth Vard, he has specifically painted her flying the Blue Ensign to commemorate a particular voyage undertaken by the author at this time. His ensign also flew from the stern of the liners *Sylvania, Saxonia, Carinthia,* and *Queen Elizabeth.* Captain Treasure Jones had finally hauled down his Blue Ensign on 9 December 1967, when he retired from the sea duty, together with his last command, the *Queen Mary.*

For the funeral of John Treasure Jones it was decided by the family that the coffin should be draped in the Blue Ensign and bear his medals, service cap and dress sword. A fitting tribute to a highly respected and consummate seaman. Initial contact with the RNR based in Southampton and Portsmouth failed to find an ensign of the suitable size. The Royal Navy at Portsmouth were also unable to assist. Finally, at the very last moment, an ensign arrived by personal courier from the RNR in Liverpool.

On 16 April 2004 the newly commissioned *QM2* left Southampton for her maiden voyage on the historical crossing to New York. As she drew away from the quay she was accompanied by many boats. One of these was a yacht, owned by David Treasure Jones, one of the three sons of Captain Treasure Jones. To honour the special occasion, flying from the backstay, was the old captain's original Blue Ensign, which had last flown with pride and honour just over thirty-six years earlier.

END NOTES

CHAPTER 1

1 The Haverfordwest Grammar School 1st Eleven Soccer Team 1920-1, trained by the Games Master, Mr Hughes (far left) is: Standing: Ian Mathias, -?- Lewis, Billy Griffiths (goal), Jack Williams (left half), Billy Miles (right back), Idris Evans (centre-half). Seated: Bily Bollom, Sidney Evans (centre-forward), Roger Morgan (captain and left back), Fred Howells, John Treasure Jones (right-half).

CHAPTER 2

1 His grandfather, Capt. Henry Sydney Williams, of 32 The Parade, Barry, stood surety in the Contract of Indentures.

2 The offices of J.C. Gould Steamship Co. were on the fourth floor of an office block, Merthyr House, James Street, Cardiff. In the photograph, Merthyr House is the building on the right-hand side. James Childs Gould had established and built up to a massive shipping and building conglomerate. Within this was the Dulcia Steam Shipping, a line which had several ships, each with a name starting with 'Grel…' such as the *Grelcaldy*.

3 Though rarely used now, the name *lascar* was used to describe a sailor from countries east of the Cape of Good Hope, particularly the Indian subcontinent, employed on European ships, from the sixteenth century until the beginning of the twentieth century. The British East India Company, for instance, recruited seamen from Yemen, Gujarat, Assam and Bengal. *Lascars* served on British ships under '*lascar* agreements'. These allowed ship owners more control than in the case in ordinary articles of agreement. The sailors could be transferred from one ship to another and retained in service for up to three years at one time.

4 Perim is an island at the most southerly point of Red Sea, in the Strait of Babel Mandeb; these days it is part of the Democratic Republic of Yemen.

5 Situated just south of Perth.

6 The Reverend Canon H.W. Brady, OBE, BA.

7 The Mission to Seafarers, which was founded in 1856, is a missionary society of the Anglican Church. It serves seafarers of all races and creeds, working through a network of full-time and part-time chaplains, staff and volunteer helpers in 230 ports around the world. In more than 100 ports it runs seafarers' centres. It is entirely dependent on voluntary contributions.

8 In the 1925 Annual Report it is recorded that:

> The staff in Buenos Aires paid 3,640 visits to ships (they had their own steam motor launch to reach those anchored off-shore) and nearly 96,000 men (equivalent to 263 per day!) responded to their invitations and visited the Institute. More than 8,000 of these have attended our services and 718 made their Communion. Nearly 3,000 officers were present at the officers' socials and over 3,000 lads joined us in the Apprentices' Socials … Canon Brady and his staff of one Assistant Chaplain and one lady worker are doing their best …

9 There was also the Mission Football League and many of the regular ship's crew enjoyed League matches during their stay in the Buenos Aires. Over 530 matches were played in 1925.

10 In the sixty-sixth Annual Report of the Missions to Seamen in 1922 Canon Brady is described as being:
... as effective as he is popular. The men and boys, cadets and officers who visit Buenos Aires have come to regard the 'Flying Angel' flag and the Canon as requisites to their happiness when lying in the stream or after they have come ashore. The Chaplain and his staff are skilled in knowing just the right thing for each of their guests, and they are equally quick in appreciating their ardour on their behalf. A guiding word, a friendly chat, a bout with the gloves, anything that will best serve, and Canon Brady has it ready.

In the book *The Great South Land* published around 1920, it states that 'his feats approach perilously close to an epic. He understands the British sailor and sees to it that the British sailor understands him. There is not a steamer plying the River Plate trade that is unknown to this worker on the waters.' A fitting tribute indeed.

11 This is probably '*Mariupol*' (also called *Zhdanov*) on the north coast of the Gulf of Taganrog, which is at the north-eastern end of the Sea of Azov.

12 In May 1925, Gould Steamships and Industrials Ltd ceased trading with a deficit in the region of £750,000, a staggering amount in those days.

In 1922, the Shipping Association's Chairman, Frederick Jones, remarked in the Annual Report:
It is not surprising to find that a number of shipping enterprises have gone into liquidation, involving heavy losses to both creditors and shareholders ... particularly those companies floated during and just after the war, when enormous capital outlay was involved in the purchase of vessels at unduly inflated prices.

CHAPTER 3

1 For details of these naval ships – refer to the Appendix.
2 HMS *Vivid*, Reserve HQ Unit, Plymouth Shore Establishment, six weeks' Gunnery Training.
3 P.R.O. reference ADM 116/2875, 2876 and 6312.

CHAPTER 4

1 The aft mast and derrick posts were removed. She was fitted with seven 5.5 guns, plus three 4in anti-aircraft guns. Painted with black hull and funnels, brown buff uppers. Two lifeboats per side.

APPENDIX 3

1 *Euripedes* was owned by G. Thompson & Co. who traded as the Aberdeen Line on the Australian route. Since there is no record of actual ownership by White Star, one can only assume that she was used on a joint service with White Star.
2 Together with the MV *Georgic*, these were the largest British 'Motor Vessels' at that time, as distinct to all the Steam Ships (SS).
3 *Vandalia* was one of 2,700 Liberty cargo ships built in the USA during the Second World War, completed as *Samaritan* by the California Shipbuilding Corp, LA. She was bought by Cunard in 1947, then sold to Greek owners in 1954 and she carried her last name *Sideris* until scrapped at Barcelona in July 1971.

APPENDIX 10

1 The term *commis* (pronounced 'commi') is used in the catering trade for a junior waiter or chef.
2 Gordon Whelan had first been his 'tiger' on the *Media*. He transferred to the *Mauretania* with the captain, and then went with him to the *Queen Mary*. As Alan mentions, the position of tiger was akin to that of a batman; they took their leave periods at the same time as their officer and moved with him from ship to ship.

Right: Belle was allowed to travel with John on the final voyage of the *Mauretania* to the scrap yard (see p. 105). Here he has issued her with the normal Certificate of Discharge.

Below: John's grandfather, Captain Henry Williams, had been captain of a sailing ship. This early photograph shows him with his motley crew, including the ship's dog.